OUR CHURCH

OUR CHURCH

*A Personal History of the
Church of England*

Roger Scruton

ATLANTIC BOOKS
LONDON

First published in hardback in Great Britain in 2012 by
Atlantic Books, an imprint of Atlantic Books Ltd.

Copyright © Roger Scruton, 2012

The moral right of Roger Scruton to be identified as
the author of this work has been asserted by him in accordance
with the Copyright, Designs and Patents Act of 1988.

The author would like to thank Faber and Faber Ltd for kind
permission to reproduce lines from T. S. Eliot's 'Little Gidding'
and from Philip Larkin's 'Church Going'.

Every effort has been made to trace or contact all
copyright-holders. The publishers will be pleased to make
good any omissions or rectify any mistakes brought to
their attention at the earliest opportunity.

3 5 7 9 10 8 6 4 2

A CIP catalogue record for this book is available
from the British Library.

978 1 84887 198 4

Printed in Great Britain by the MPG Books Group

Atlantic Books
An imprint of Atlantic Books Ltd
Ormond House
26–27 Boswell Street
London WC1N 3JZ

Contents

OUR CHURCH

Preface

This book is not an academic history of the Anglican Church or a systematic account, still less a justification, of its message. It is a personal record of what the Church of England has meant to me, and a tribute to its peaceful and creative presence in our national life. I hope it will be read with interest not only by Anglicans, but also by Christians of other denominations, as well as by non-Christians and non-believers. For it seems to me that our country is greatly misunderstood by the many influential people who fail to see that our national church remains part of its identity, and the key to its past.

Previous drafts of this book have been read by Pat Burke, Mark Dooley, Alicja Gęścińska, Bob Grant and Andrew Lenox-Conyngham, and I am grateful to them for their advice, criticism and suggestions. Here and there I have drawn on material already published in my book *England: An Elegy*, which contains a brief chapter on English religion, and I am grateful to the publishers of that book, Continuum, for permission to use short passages of the text.

Malmesbury, March 2012

ONE

Religion, Faith and Church

Since the 'Glorious Revolution' of 1688 the English way of life has been often under the novelist's microscope. And we, looking into that microscope, discover that there is no more curious aspect of the English than their attitude to religion. While the Church of England has been all-important in shaping the lives of the English people, the Christian religion has been, since the late seventeenth century, only a subdued presence in their lives. If Jane Austen's young clergymen were training for the army rather than the priesthood, their relations with the women who assess them would remain unaltered. And if the livings and prebends, the bishoprics and deaconries, over which Trollope's characters so relentlessly strive, were lucrative situations in the entertainment industry, their social motives would hardly be changed. The philosopher David Hume remarked on the indifference of the English in matters of religion, and George Orwell repeated the observation in his wartime essay *The Lion and the Unicorn*. A modern observer could be forgiven for thinking that the Christian faith was some kind of mistake that the English once made, from the effects of which they freed themselves in the tumultuous civil conflicts of the seventeenth century. The Church that survived those violent times was one part of the system of English government, with no spiritual claims beyond the minimum required by social tranquillity. And the godless society of modern England, some might say, is exactly what we should expect, when the Church allies itself so closely with the State that it cannot afford the cost of religious passion.

Understandable though such an observation would be, it is not entirely accurate. The England that I knew as a child in the fifties was not godless. Most people declared some kind of Christian attachment, and churchgoing, though a minority pursuit, was not a target of ridicule. Those intellectuals who publicly questioned the dogmas of the established church were not evangelical atheists of the Richard Dawkins kind, but spirited agnostics like Jacob Bronowski, who conceded that they could not be entirely sure about God's non-existence, even if they were pretty sure about everything else. The Anglican Church was represented in school assemblies across the nation, and the Bible was widely read both in the class-room and at home. Most people responded to the rare official enquiries about their religion with the harmless formula 'C. of E.'. When, at the coronation of Queen Elizabeth II, the Church stepped into the centre of public life, few people doubted its right to do so, and even the most grudging of unbelievers was moved by the spectacle of the young Queen as she humbly accepted what she regarded as a sacred duty, and in doing so made it sacred.

I was nine years old at the time, and followed the coronation ceremony on the black and white television that our maternal grandmother had provided for the purpose. Our father was a social-ist, a republican and an atheist. Yet he too watched the ceremony, regarding it as the sole justification to date of this contraption through which the world of morons had intruded into our house. He and our mother sat in silence, sometimes wiping away their tears. The rituals and words that they witnessed embodied the spirit of England, for whose sake they had made their share of wartime sacrifices. Here were the robes and crowns and diadems, the bishops, deans and archdeacons, the Lords Privy Seal, Great Chamberlain, High Chancellor and High Constable, the whole pack of cards floating on words and music imbued with that peculiar Anglican dignity, which is the dignity of a people who can never witness a ceremony without thinking of the mess that will need clearing up afterwards. But for a precious moment, as the illusions stepped down from the looking glass and occupied our ordinary living room, it seemed that all the recent sacrifices had been worth it.

Such moments in the life of a nation are rare. But they have their counterparts in the lives of individuals. Like nations, human beings pass through times of transition and proof, during which they depend on a validation that must come to them from others. Birth, coming of age, marriage and death are transitions in the life of the individual that are also transitions in the life of the tribe. In pre-modern societies these moments are marked by 'rites of passage', which lift them out of our day-to-day transactions and endow them with a transcendental meaning.[1] They are, to use T. S. Eliot's words, 'points of intersection of the timeless / With time': moments at which eternity is 'made manifest' in rituals that alert us to the fact that far more is at stake in our lives than the vacillating course of human appetite. It is only thus that we can become fully aware of eternal meanings, and those who scoff at ceremonies register their scepticism towards the transcendental, which can show itself publicly in no other way. It is undeniable that this scepticism is now part of the English character. But it coexists with a certain curiosity towards the transcendental, and a desire to imagine it on the English model, as a place where we might be at home – an eternal *Wind in the Willows*, governed by a ghostly pack of cards.

If we are to understand the Church of England as I and many of my generation have known it, we need to recognize that religion is not simply a matter of believing a few abstract metaphysical propositions that stand shaking and vulnerable before the advance of modern science. Religion is a way of life, involving customs and ceremonies that validate what matters to us, and which reinforce the attachments by which we live. It is both a faith and a form of membership, in which the destiny of the individual is bound up with that of a community. And it is a way in which the ordinary, the everyday and the unsurprising are rescued from the flow of time and re-made as sacrosanct. A religion has its accumulations of dogma; but dogmas make no real sense when detached from the community that adheres to them, being not neutral statements of fact but collective bids for salvation.

The very word 'faith' speaks to this position: it suggests that, beyond a certain point, we must *trust* in something, take something *on trust*, cease to look for proofs or to conduct experiments, but simply receive the certainties of faith by allowing ourselves to be open to them, and open also to the grace of God. Rational theology attempts to give an account of God, man and their relationship that is intrinsically reasonable. Such a theology we find in Augustine and Aquinas; in Ibn Sina (Avicenna) and Ibn Rushd (Averroës); and in Moses Ben Maimon (Maimonides). Those thinkers believed their separate faiths to be connected by chains of analogy and inference to a rationally justified picture of the world, in which the place of God and God's relation to man can be sketched in plausible outline. But they also believed that without the revelation, by which the fundamental bond of trust is forged, rational theology is useless. And about the revelation they did not agree.

For when it comes to the transcendental, trust is all we can give. Stories of idols and icons who are beaten when they fail to produce rain remind us of the absurdity of attempting to influence a super-natural power by offering merely earthly rewards and punishments.[2] All we can offer is ourselves – to make a gift of ourselves; and that is precisely what faith consists in – the assertion that '*totus tuus sum*',[3] I am wholly yours. Mystics like St Teresa of Avila, St John of the Cross and Rumi express this idea with erotic allusions and metaphors. Others are content merely to emphasize the connection between faith and trust, and between trust and surrender. Note, however, that '*islam*' does not mean surrender to a conquering dictator, but the humble acknowledgement that, whatever you take for great, God is greater.[4]

From faith springs prayer. You can believe in God without believing in the efficacy of prayer: such was the position adopted by

Spinoza, for example. But Spinoza did not believe in the supernatural; God for him was simply another name for nature, conceived as a whole – a position that was at first condemned as atheism, and subsequently praised (by Goethe among others) as pantheism. As soon as you acknowledge the existence of a supernatural being that can have an influence over your life, either here below or in some unknown hereafter, prayer becomes inevitable.

But then there is the question: how do I pray? This question has preoccupied people from the beginning of recorded time. Early religious texts contain prayers that define the form of words, the epithets, and the kinds of requests with which the gods are rightly addressed. We have striking examples in the Egyptian Book of the Dead, the Psalms, the Vedas and the Homeric hymns. And they all reinforce the perception that prayer is difficult, requiring special words, a special frame of mind, and an attempt to comprehend aspects of yourself that are hidden from everyday perception. Prayer is not simply asking for something: it is coming into relation with the supernatural. 'Just as in earthly life,' wrote Kierkegaard, 'lovers long for the moment when they are able to breathe forth their love for each other, to let their souls blend in a soft whisper, so the mystic longs for the moment when in prayer he can, as it were, creep into God.'[5]

This 'creeping into God' is something that saints and mystics may achieve spontaneously, as infants crawl to the breast. But for the rest of us it is something we must learn. It involves a momentary withdrawal from the natural world, so as to project our thoughts beyond it. That is why special phrases, liturgies and hallowed language are necessary: they are the guarantee that we are addressing a transcendental Other, and not just talking somewhat pompously to ourselves. This is the difference between a prayer and a wish; and also suggests that the life of prayer is part of the collective surrender, the lapse into membership, to which every religion invites its following.

The great sociologists who put the study of religion on a scientific footing – Émile Durkheim and Max Weber – were aware of those thoughts, and did much to endow them with theoretical underpinnings. But neither of them took much notice of the Anglican Church or recognized its inimitable contribution to the national life of which it was, and to some extent still is, a part. In this book I want to explore some aspects of this unique institution, and to show what is at stake in its current decline. I write as someone who has throughout his life drifted in and out of his mother Church, and who still recognizes the Anglican Communion as his home. But I hope that what I say will be of interest and relevance to all who acknowledge the importance of religion in human life, and who have felt in themselves the trauma that our society is suffering, as its traditional forms of worship fade from public view.

The Abrahamic religions make demands of their adherents under the two broad headings introduced by St Paul in his Epistle to the Romans and deployed for purposes of his own by Martin Luther: the headings of Faith and Works (*pistis kai erga*). Faith is not simply subscribing to a list of doctrines, as though ticking the boxes of a questionnaire. Works are not blind obedience to a catalogue of divine requests. Faith and works take on their religious character when they fill the soul. Thus Muslims believe that the Koran is the word of God, revealed to Muhammad, and that all its imperatives are binding. They commit to witnessing repeatedly to this (the *shahadah*), to reciting the five daily prayers, to performing acts of charity (*zakat*), to obeying the fast of Ramadan and the rituals of pilgrimage. But those requirements do not make a pious Muslim. You must also *bring God into your life*. The commitments of faith and works must be constantly refreshed and renewed, as though you were coming for the first time to see the truth of the revelation, and the beauty of God's commands. And the equivalent demand is made of the devout Christian, who is required not just to repeat the forms of prayer and worship, but 'to walk in the way of the Cross'.

To bring God into your life is not a simple matter. Special words, special actions, special signs are needed. Faith is a form of consecration; but one person's consecration is another person's sacrilege. Swift, that model Anglican clergyman, wrote that no wars are 'so furious as those occasioned by difference in opinion, especially if it be in things indifferent'.[6] The decision to bow or not to bow at the mention of Christ's name, to kneel or not to kneel at Communion, to make or not to make the sign of the cross – all such decisions have, at one time or another, divided Christians into warring factions, notwithstanding a shared belief in the meaning of Christ's sacrifice, and a shared acceptance of the great commandment to love your neighbour as yourself.

Rationalists and atheists look on such disputes with scorn, believing them to be proof that religion rots the minds and the morals of those who adhere to it. But they tend to forget that wars of religion are the price paid for the peace of religion. Peace never makes the headlines, and occupies only a footnote in the history books. But peace, like war, erupts from places in the human psyche that are outside the control of reason. Rituals and doctrines become prominent in war because they are prominent in peace: they are the way in which we build trust between strangers, and a sign given from each to each that we belong together and can stand side by side in the face of our common danger.

This casts further light on the nature of faith. Religious beliefs shape the allegiance and coherence of a community, and opinions are judged heretical when they threaten to fragment the community. Hence, as Swift noticed, large differences of opinion are less threatening than small ones. When someone differs completely from me as to whether God exists, or whether there really was someone called Muhammad to whom the Koran was revealed, then I may feel that he is no real threat to me, since he is beyond the pale of my community. He belongs to another community and another faith, and the only question is whether our two communities can live side by side in a peaceful way – the question confronted in one way by the Ottoman Empire, in another way by European societies since the Reformation.

If, however, we agree about everything except whether the Holy Spirit proceeds from the Father or whether the Holy Spirit proceeds from the Father through the Son, the result is a schism – the schism that split the Christian Church into that of Rome and that of Constantinople. And the smaller the difference the more intense the dispute. The Russian Orthodox Church was split in the nineteenth century around the question whether you should make the sign of the cross with two fingers or with three – the dispute between the Old and the Young Believers. The dispute led to massacres and pillages, and fatally undermined the stability of Russia, preparing the way for the Bolshevik revolution. Likewise Sunnite and Shi'ite disagree over the succession to the Prophet, while accepting the same Holy Book, the same law and the same customs. This tiny disagreement, of no significance to an outsider, is sufficient to inspire genocidal warfare between those whom it divides.

When a doctrine or practice has become foundational to a community, it has been placed beyond question, and the person who continues to question it must be expelled. Religions aim for a state in which worship, ritual and doctrine are settled until the end of time. They aim to put themselves *beyond history*. If they have a history nevertheless, it is a history of excommunications. And to recognize this, while adhering to a faith of one's own, is hard. But this hard task is one that Christ himself imposed on us. The parable of the Good Samaritan instructs us to look for common ground, rather than the evidence of heresy. And it is partly in this spirit that the Anglican Church succeeded in reconciling the demands of faith and the imperative of national unity at the end of the seventeenth century.

We should never underestimate the human need for membership. We are social beings, who are incomplete when we are unable to identify the community that is *ours*. We long for home and homecoming; our images of peace are also images of settlement; and all our ideals are informed by the need to receive and to give some form of love. It would be highly implausible to think that religion was something entirely detached from this need for membership, rather than a way of providing for it: in this Durkheim is surely right.[7] But it would also be wrong to assume that just any way of providing for the need qualifies as a religion. Religious experience is a *specific* way of encountering and solving the problem of membership, and one that engages another and deeper aspect of the human psyche, which is the recognition of the sacred and the associated fear of profanation.

Religious rituals do not work like passwords or badges. They renew us, cleanse us of the real and imagined guilt that attends the proximity of others' judgement. In short, they are purifications. It is impossible to understand the religious urge if we do not grasp this point. Religion expresses a profound and species-wide longing for purity, a longing to be 'cleansed' of the many and minute transgressions that are the price we pay for consciousness.[8] This idea – conveyed to Jews, Christians and Muslims in the story of the Fall – is not an arbitrary addition to the store of religious dogma. It is the heart of religion in all its forms and an inescapable part of the human condition. Some people feel this longing less strongly than others. There are heroes of guilt, like Al-Ghazzali, Kierkegaard and St Thérèse de Lisieux, for whom the burden defines the direction of their lives. And there are the ordinary, complacent people like you and me, for whom the quest for purity is an irritation, something to be got out of the way through some convenient ritual in which we can, for a blessed moment, own up to our condition and let the light shine in. Yet all of us, whatever our spiritual laxity, experience the constant need to refresh ourselves, to be purged of our transgressions, and to begin again with a clean slate. The primordial cry of the religious soul is that of Psalm 51: 'Purge me with hyssop, and I shall be clean: wash me, and I shall be whiter than snow... Create in me a clean heart, O God; and renew a right spirit within me.' And the Psalmist goes on to add the stunning verse that says more clearly than anything else just what religion is about: 'The sacrifices of God are a broken spirit; a broken and a contrite heart, O God, thou wilt not despise.'

The ideas of purity and purification are not simply obscure residues of our evolutionary past, which mystics and magicians manipulate for their own nefarious purposes. They lie on the very surface of consciousness, and have shaped the genres and subjects of European art. The purification of love is the dominant theme of medieval romance; the purging of corruption and the restoration of moral purity form the subject-matter of Shakespeare's great last plays – for example, *The Winter's Tale* and *The Tempest*. In Mozart's *Magic Flute* Tamino and Pamina are purified by the rites of Sarastro's temple, and so made fit for marriage. In Dostoevsky's *Crime and Punishment* the prostitute Sonya retains the purity of soul for which Raskolnikov hungers, and her faithful adherence through all his trials purges him at last of guilt. In those and a thousand other examples, we find artists paying tribute to the search for purity, as something both distinctive of the human condition and at the root of moral hope.

The reason for this dominant role of purity in human thinking is not hard to find. The distinction between self and other is a crux in the life of reason that no mere animal must face. All around us are people more successful, more talented, more attractive and more powerful than ourselves, and in all our most important endeavours we desire what another desires and fight for its possession. But we are also dependent on others, and need to renew our mutual attach-ment. This problem – which René Girard has characterized as the problem of 'mimetic desire' – is not soluble by rational discussion.[9] It demands a repeated change of life, a repeated washing away of resentment. And religious ritual provides those necessary things – helping us for a moment to stand in the light of eternity, from which we can return duly cleansed into the here and now. How this is done, and what explains the power of the ritual that is supposed to accomplish it, are questions to which Girard gives a disturbing answer, and one that I touch on in the conclusion to this book. But we shall not understand the Christian religion, in terms acceptable to an enquiring modern mind, still less will we understand the Anglican Church, if we do not see them as respectively general and specific solutions to the collective inheritance of guilt and resentment. Thus the 'familiar compound ghost' of *Four Quartets* summarizes the 'gifts reserved for age':

> And last, the rending pain of re-enactment
> Of all that you have done, and been; the shame
> Of motives late revealed, and the awareness
> Of things ill done and done to others' harm
> Which once you took for exercise of virtue.

15

Then fools' approval stings, and honour stains.
From wrong to wrong the exasperated spirit
Proceeds, unless restored by that refining fire
Where you must move in measure, like a dancer.

The 'refining fire' is an allusion to Dante's description of Purgatory. But Eliot is referring more generally to the purifying discipline of penance, in which we offer up 'a broken and a contrite heart'.

The longing for purity does not stand alone in the human psyche. Mysteries are contained in stories, which relieve them of their eeriness and invite them into the world of human events. These stories, which begin as myth, often end as dogma. They become systematic accounts of the human condition, laying down a path to salvation and inviting the bewildered soul into relation with another and higher world. These stories will offer solutions to the mystery of the individual existence, by enfolding it in the larger mystery of a created world.

In developing its account of the human condition, early Christianity was helped by the multicultural nature of the Roman Empire, which brought the intellectual legacy of Greece to bear on the spiritual *Angst* of the Jews. From Greek philosophy came the idea of the infinite, eternal and self-created God, the being outside time on whom the temporal order depends. From the Torah of the Jews came the story of a people chosen by God, and burdened with his commandments. It is common among those who take an anthropological view of things to see Christianity as containing a synthesis of those two monotheisms – that of the Aristotelian schools, for whom God lies above and beyond the world, to be reached only by the frail ladders of abstract argument; and that of the Torah, in which God roams the world of mortals, never wholly or clearly revealed to them, but brimful of interest in their doings and letting slip from time to time the extent of his favour and his wrath.

Christ came among us, the early Christians thought, in order to replace a false notion of religious purity, as a condition secured by outward obedience to often nonsensical rules, with a truer and more inward discipline. God is not the private possession of the Jews, nor is he circumscribed by fussy legalisms. He is the universal God of love, who promises eternal life, and who reveals to us, through Christ, the two commandments 'on which hang all the law and the prophets': to love God entirely, and to love your neighbour as your-self. Just what this involves was made clear by Christ himself, who made, on the cross, 'a full, perfect, and sufficient sacrifice, oblation, and satisfaction, for the sins of the whole world' – as it says in the Book of Common Prayer.

The God of the New Testament is, therefore, revealed not as law but as love: the love granted to all who suffer from the primeval guilt that is the price of freedom. Christ is the 'lamb of God, that taketh away the sins of the world'. He is the sacrificial offering, who brings love and forgiveness to his tormentors. He is the Word of God, despised and rejected by those whom he comes to save. And how can he be these things if he is merely a prophet like any other, whose message could have been conveyed by another person in another form? Thanks to the stories of the Resurrection (six already collected by St Paul in I Corinthians 15), thanks to the recorded miracles and the stunned reports of Christ's presence, the first Christians found themselves ineluctably driven to the thought of Christ as the Son of God. And from that thought sprang another: that Christ is identical with God – he is the revelation of God in the flesh, the Word made flesh, and hence 'the point of intersection of the timeless / With time'.

The doctrine of the Incarnation provided, to the first Christians, the full explanation of the momentous experience through which they had lived. And at the beginning of his Gospel St John provided the concepts with which the central mystery of the Christian religion could be both expressed as doctrine and enacted as sacred ritual. Jesus Christ was not just a mediator between God and man, but a revelation of God *to* man. The Word was made flesh and dwelt among us. And in order to account for the continued presence of the Holy Spirit, the early Christians expanded the doctrine of the Incarnation to that of the Trinity – God in three Persons, who is yet one thing.

The Trinity is both the foundational doctrine and the central mystery of the Christian religion, and one on which the Anglican Church has its own hard-won perspective. At the heart of all the upheavals that have shaped the forms and the institutions of the Christian faith lie disputes about this doctrine, and about the sacrament – the Eucharist – that is its sensory expression. It is, therefore, necessary to say something about how these disputes arose and, more importantly, how they were resolved.

The faith in Christ's divinity sustained the Church during the centuries of persecution and comforted the martyrs in their final moments. During this period the sects and heresies proliferated underground, and the doctrine of the Trinity was believed and the Eucharist celebrated without any common determination as to what they really mean. With the conversion of the Emperor Constantine all that changed, and one of the most important of Constantine's acts as Emperor was to summon a council of the whole Church – the Council of Nicaea (AD 325). The ostensible occasion was the preaching of the Alexandrian Arius, who taught that the second Person of the Trinity is not fully God, since he has a beginning in time and is subject to change, while God is unchangeable and eternal. This 'Arian heresy' was rejected and anathematized, and – significantly – it was the Emperor who wrote to Arius demanding his submission. The council also gave birth to the Nicene Creed, which (subsequently augmented at the Council of Constantinople) remains a fundamental statement of Christian doctrine:

> I believe in one God the Father Almighty,
> Maker of Heaven and Earth,
> And of all things visible and invisible:
> And in one Lord Jesus Christ, the only-begotten Son of God,
> Begotten of his Father before all worlds...

The disputes continued, and another heresy – that of Nestorius – denied the identity of Jesus Christ with the Son, arguing that Jesus was united with the Son, but in himself of a human and temporal nature. The Nestorian heresy was put down at the Council of

Chalcedon, which resolved all the relevant disputes with the doctrine that Christ is one person with two natures – expressing the point in terms largely dug from the philosophical remains of pagan Greece. In an extended and deeply pondered work, St Augustine had already developed his own theory of the Trinity, arguing that no other view of God could make proper sense of the Gospel story. Augustine's *De Trinitate* argued that it is right to use the Latin '*persona*', in the place of the Greek '*hypostasis*', and opened the way to the idea that God's condition is essentially inter-personal. Each of the divine Persons serves the other and is served by him, and all of them are bound in one substance, whose essence is love – not the love that the Greeks called *eros*, but the *agape* of St Paul's First Epistle to the Corinthians. Erotic love, according to Plato, begins in attachment to earthly things, and aspires beyond them to the realm of things divine. Christian charity, by contrast, begins in Heaven, and comes down to us as a gift that we share with our neighbours.[10]

The disputes about the Trinity reflect two deep questions that all monotheistic religions must face: how is God revealed to us? And how do we discover what he wants? Summarizing the debates in the tenth century, the Muslim apologist 'Abd al-Jabbar pointed to the absurdity, as he saw it, of the idea that God became Man in the way that Jesus did – the absurdity that 'he who is beyond time should also begin'.[11] And he searches the pages of the Gospel of St Paul and of the documents of the Christian councils in order to show the confusions that result from the belief that eternity and time can be conjoined in one person. However, at the time that al-Jabbar was writing the Muslims had the very same problem. If God had revealed himself in the Koran, then did the holy recitals come into being at a particular time, as the Muʿtazalites (of whom al-Jabbar was one) claimed, so as to be addressed to particular people in a particular context and, therefore, open to interpretation by those who came after them and whose circumstances had changed? Or was the Koran, as the Ash'arites argued, eternal and uncreated, so as to allow no amendment and no reinterpretation? On one understanding the Koran speaks to us in dialogue, on the other it lies beyond our reach, like a star shining from the edge of space. Either way, we are in need of that 'point of intersection of the timeless / With time' that Christians discover in the person of Christ. And it is the absence of this precious thing, some may say, that has landed Islam in its peculiar modern predicament, of absolute obedience to an eternal law that has lost connection with a changing world.

The difficult points of doctrine and practice that troubled the early Church were not resolved by consulting some Koran-like infallible source, even though the Church accepted the Bible as the 'Word of God'. They were settled by discussion in council, among bishops who called the Holy Spirit to their aid. The discussions were often rowdy, and during the councils bishops were regularly attacked and injured – one even killed – by their more hot-headed opponents. But it was discussion, not violence, that determined the outcome, and discussion conducted in the presence of the Emperor, who maintained order as best he could. Moreover it was the Emperors, and not the bishops, who imposed the results. For the Emperors regarded the uniformity of religious belief and practice as fundamental to the stability of their government, while conceding that it was bishops, not Emperors, who had the business of deciding what uniformity consists in.

From the beginning, therefore, Christianity emerged as a conciliar religion, in which doctrines are not taken ready-made from the store of revelation but discovered through discussion, criticism and reform. And Christian religious leaders tended to act in concert with the secular power, while maintaining their doctrinal prerogative. Those two features endured, and came again into prominence when the Anglican Church finally broke from Rome in the sixteenth century. And they mark the places at which the contrast between Christianity and Islam is most pronounced. Since the triumph of Ash'arite theology in the eleventh century of our era it has been understood in Sunni Islam that the will of God has been pronounced for all time, that there can be no theological discoveries and no revisions of the Holy Law through human council – in short that 'the gate of *ijtihad* [reflective interpretation] is closed'. Furthermore it has been the goal of Sunni Islam to impose the Holy Law (the *shari'ah*) upon its followers, and to release them from all the institutions of secular government that might stand in the way of God's will. I have argued elsewhere that this contrast between the institutional and secular approach of Christianity and the unmediated and theocratic approach of Islam is at the root of the tensions that we are living through today.[12]

Islam must be understood, therefore, as a completely different form of religious practice from that which shaped our country, and which achieved quiescence at last in our national church. The differences that matter most and that define the real nature of the tension between the two faiths are not the differences of doctrine, significant though they are, but differences in the form of membership that they promise. Membership for a Christian means membership of a church. Membership for a Muslim means submission to the will of Allah, as revealed in the Koran and the *sunnah*, and no institution has any authority that is not derived from that source. The Christians have their sacred text too; but it is a text that is open to interpretation. Christians believe that the mission of Jesus was not to burden the Jewish people with new additions to their fussy system of religious rules. On the contrary, his mission was to call people to discipleship, by creating an *ecclesia* – an assembly – promising that, when people gather together in his name, he too would be there among them. St Paul gave form and substance to this assembly, which grew under his guidance as an entity distinct from its members, one with its own rules and laws, and with offices that embodied and preserved the Apostolic Succession begun by Christ, when he entrusted his church to St Peter. The Church of England believes itself to be maintaining that Apostolic Succession to this day.

Christ was a subject of the Roman Empire. He shaped his mission in full knowledge that he lived under a secular rule of law, which tolerated religions of all kinds, provided they accepted the supremacy of the secular authorities in matters of civil government. In the parable of the Tribute Money Christ summarizes what was to become an enduring theme of Christian political thought, calling on his disciples to 'render unto Caesar what is Caesar's, and to God what is God's' – in other words, to obey the secular law in public life, and to obey the commandments of religion in all matters to do with salvation and the world to come. He clearly assumed that, properly formulated, the two jurisdictions need not conflict.

Different Christian traditions have interpreted this parable in different ways. But the Roman Catholic Church incorporated it in the fifth century, when Pope Gelasius wrote to the Emperor Anastasius declaring that God had given to mankind 'two swords' for their good government, that of religion, wielded by the Church, and that of secular law, wielded by the temporal power. The many subsequent conflicts between Church and State, Pope and Emperor, religious observance and secular law may suggest that the doctrine of the two swords describes an ideal to which in practice human communities have found it all but impossible to conform. But it should be said, first, that it is an ideal that has no place in Islamic theology or political thought, and secondly, that it is an ideal that over time has worked its way downwards from the 'kingdom of ends' into the world of means, and that the separation of religious from secular jurisdiction is now to be observed throughout the Western world. Indeed, it is to be counted as one of the great achievements of the Christian faith, and one that is owed to the Church's Roman origins. It has from time to time seemed as though the religious jurisdiction of our country has been absorbed by the secular; and it is undeniable that the two jurisdictions were, during the sixteenth and seventeenth centuries, more closely intertwined than was good for either of them. But the subsequent history of the Anglican Church is that of a religious institution steadily freeing itself from the secular government to which it is nominally subject, while retaining a position in society that is authorized and endorsed by the secular law.

Until the conversion of the Emperor Constantine the Church led a shadowy existence, often assembling in secret, frequently persecuted, and the object of widespread suspicion among those who did not share its faith. Once legalized, however, the Church could enjoy the protection of the Roman law, arguably the greatest intellectual achievement of the ancient world. The Roman law was secular: it made a place for religion, but did not impose it. And it managed the claims of the religious life through the concept of the corporate person, which comes before the law as a single entity, owner of privileges and duties, able to hold property in its own right, and to lay down rules for the election and dismissal of its officers. In other words, the Church emerged from the catacombs as a *person*, enjoying the protection of the law. The structure was already in place that would grant legal reality to her spiritual claims, as the body and the bride of Christ. (The custom of referring to the Church as 'she' reflects this.) The corporate person can impose discipline on its members, and also answer for them collectively. It can make contracts and promises on behalf of people who, as mere individuals, are incompetent to speak for anyone but themselves. It can be a full and equal partner in the affairs of state, and the representative of its members in any negotiations in which their spiritual needs are at stake.

No equivalent of this exists in Islamic law, which has never recognized corporate personality, and which regards all collectives as legal fictions. This is one of the reasons why Islamic sects have failed to negotiate solutions to their conflicts. Quite literally, they have no one who can speak for them. For if there is something that could speak for a religious community, it is not some one member of it, however highly placed, but the corporate person that can represent the community as a whole. The absence of corporate personality and the belief that secular law has no independent validity have between them made it difficult for Islam to reconcile itself to the most important feature of democratic politics, which is the priority of secular and territorial jurisdiction as a form of government, and the presence of religious communities within the jurisdiction on negotiated terms.[13] The story of the Church of England is the story of how *we* achieved those things, on this island and across the wide Empire that once was governed from it.

Throughout the early conflicts over the Pelagian, Arian and Nestorian heresies, Christians were aware of the fragility of their new community, and of the need to protect it from internal dissent and fragmentation. They were persuaded that there could be only *one* church, namely the church entrusted by Christ to St Peter, and that this church should be *the* Church. (Hence the use, which I shall for the most part follow, of the capital 'C' when referring to it.) This Church is not just a corporate person. It, or rather she, is a spiritual person, variously described as the Bride of Christ, the Body of Christ, Holy Mother Church, the Communion of the Saints, and in any case something more than just one corporate person among others. Her relation with her Founder is more intimate, more spiritually tremendous, than any merely human relation, for she is endowed with the Holy Spirit, and is literally an aspect or agent of

God. This conception of the Church invites awe among those who accept it, and rebellion among those who do not. In any case, the contest over the claim to embody it is at the root of the great schism that separated the Orthodox from the Roman Churches, both of which claim to be the presence on earth of the Body of Christ, and both of which describe themselves as '*katholikos*' – that is, universal. The Church of England too has retained that description, and has claimed to be the valid successor of St Peter, though whether the Church of England admits all other 'catholic' churches to that dignity has never been clear.

The Church of England is heir to the conciliar tradition and to the alliance between secular government and doctrinal conformity that was forged in the early councils. Hence it has had little difficulty, since the end of the seventeenth-century wars of religion, in both asserting its exclusive constitutional privileges, and in politely giving way to those who challenge them. It is indeed an achievement of Christianity that it has taken the need for spiritual membership and turned it towards the Other who does not belong. The vision of the suffering God, who makes the supreme sacrifice, lies always before the Christian; he is invited to rehearse the sacrifice that redeemed him; he is enjoined to forgive his enemies and to turn the other cheek to those who torment him; and he is encouraged to solve his conflicts through discussion, and in a spirit of charity.

It is to perpetuate that approach to life, all churches maintain, that Christ bestowed his trust on St Peter, and the real work of a church, whatever its doctrine, is to encourage its members on the path laid down for them by the God of love. Nietzsche saw

Christian meekness as the spirit of resentment, turned against itself. In a thorough examination of this claim, the German philosopher Max Scheler showed beyond doubt that neighbour-love (*agape*), as Christianity conceives it, is not the effect of resentment but its cure – perhaps its only cure.[14] Rather than revisit Scheler's arguments, however, I shall merely point to the history of the Anglican compromise, and say that *res ipsa loquitur* – the thing speaks for itself.

The early Church was not planned: it arose by 'an invisible hand' from the many attempts to determine the requirements of 'faith and works'. By the time philosophers turned their attention to it, the Church was an established institution with an accumulation of ecclesiastical laws and offices, of authorities and councils, of titles and properties, of orders and privileges, which had evolved without being prompted into consciousness by the fact of competition. The most important medieval discussion – Marsilio of Padua's *Defensor Pacis* (1324) – argues plausibly that, if the Holy Spirit shows itself among us, it is first and foremost in the councils that bring us together in the pursuit of truth and salvation. And a council does not give orders only: it listens, discusses, consults those who are affected by its decisions, and acts not for the good of some leader but for the good of the whole.

Marsilio's conciliar theory was directed against the contemporary Papacy, which, he believed, laid claim to an earthly power to which it was not entitled. He saw the Church as one corporate citizen among others, which had its own sphere of authority, but which could not usurp the territory rightly claimed by secular lawmakers. Despite its conciliatory nature, Marsilio's is still a theory of the *one* Church, the Body of Christ, the great spiritual organism that admits of no plural, and which is not, in the end, a human creation. It is precisely this claim to uniqueness that exposed the Church to the attacks of reformers and purists. Throughout the Middle Ages the Church had to contend with protests and threats prompted by its own vices and corruption, but never could it respond by inviting the critics to set up a rival church of their own. Every schism – even that which led to the existence of two Popes, one in Rome and one in Avignon – was regarded as an injury to the *one* Church, rather than the creation of another. It was only at the Reformation that the idea began to be seriously entertained that churches could be as well made as inherited. The reformers, whether or not they were conscious of this, wanted to *create* churches; and therefore they wanted to know just what it is that makes an institution into a church, rather than, say, a family, a club, a business, an army or a school.

At the risk of grossly simplifying, we can divide the reformers into those who set about developing a wholly new conception of the church as an institution both divinely guided and humanly created, and those who turned away from that task in order to reform the one Church, retaining as many of its trappings as seemed compatible with holiness, while correcting abuses, and returning to the true source of religious authority in the Bible. Of the first kind of reformer John Calvin (1509–64) was pre-eminent; of the second Martin Luther (1483–1546). Calvin's establishment of his new church in Geneva was accompanied by a thorough thinking through of every aspect of Christian devotion and discipleship – not the doctrines and forms of worship only, but the laws and institutions of a Christian society. In Calvin's Geneva, State and Church coalesced, and the *Institutes* established for the government of the second were very soon being used to govern the first. But Calvin remained true to what he considered to be the first principle of the Christian *ecclesia*, which is that the Christian Church is an assembly of equals, which may enjoy the ministrations of a priest, but which does not permit the accumulation of offices and pomp displayed by the Roman Catholic episcopate. And because of the purism and comprehensiveness of his approach, Calvin probably exerted a greater influence over the early English reformers than did Luther.

The Church of Rome emerged from the Middle Ages in possession of a 'Magisterium', to which all questions of doctrine could be referred, and in which the apostolic authority of the Church was fortified by the rational theology of St Thomas Aquinas and the scholastics. The Protestant churches had no such doctrinal legacy, nor did they want one, believing that through a judicious combination of abstract speculation and worldly pomp, the Roman Church had been able to conceal its departure from the path laid down by Christ. Calvin replaced the authority of bishops with the authority of God's Word. And instead of a philosophical theology he sought a Biblical theology, in which doctrines would be derived from the Gospel revelation rather than from tradition or from abstract philosophical proofs. Like Luther he believed in justification by faith and he sought, through faith, a direct encounter with the redeeming Christ. St Paul and St Augustine, rather than the intricacies of medieval theology, were his guides; but he recognized nevertheless the need for system. Indeed, it is the promise of system that drew the English reformers – including Thomas Cranmer, who was to become Henry VIII's Archbishop – into Calvin's orbit.

Calvin believed that there is no salvation outside the Church; but he distinguished the Invisible Church, whose head is Jesus, from the Visible Church – the human institution that constantly falls short of the founding purpose. The Church of Rome had upheld seven sacraments: Baptism, the Eucharist, Holy Orders, Penance, Confirmation, Marriage and Unction. Calvin retained only Baptism and the Eucharist – the two for which there is Gospel authority. Priesthood, in the Calvinist church, received no sacramental privileges, being simply the way in which the faith is taught. The Apostolic Succession, the consecration of bishops and clergy, the laying on of hands and the hierarchical pomp of penance and confirmation were all dismissed as hocus pocus, irrelevant to the one critical matter, which is faith itself. Calvin identified the Incarnation – the revelation of God in Christ – as the premise of faith, the thing to be understood by all believers. Although, in his later years, he became a petulant guardian of the Church that he had founded, Calvin's early editions of the *Institutes* reveal a candid and honest attempt to think things through that made a deep impression on the English divines. They were drawn to Calvin's vision of a wholly new form of religious community, cleansed of worldly corruption, in which everything believed, and everything performed, would have the direct authority of the Gospels.

There were other and more controversial aspects of Calvinism, however, and one in particular – the Calvinist doctrine of predestination, according to which salvation is bestowed on those already elected by God – profoundly affected the development of the Anglican compromise. This doctrine (foreshadowed in St Augustine and perhaps also in St Paul) was not at first emphasized by Calvin. But by the time Calvinism was adopted as the official religion of the new Dutch Republic, predestination had become a kind of controlling principle, the test of membership in a church that existed largely as a club for those who didn't really need it, since they were already saved. Protesting against the absurdity of this, the theologian Jacobus Arminius (1560–1609) argued that Christ died for all sinners, and that God's grace, offered to every penitent believer, is the sole and sufficient guarantee of salvation. The followers of Arminius (the Remonstrants) were anathematized and cast out of the Dutch Church, and for a time Spinoza, who had been similarly anathematized by the Synagogue, lived among them. But despite official persecution their influence spread, so that Arminianism became a recognized form of Protestant belief, and one that was to have a lasting impact on the English reformed churches.

The Reformation envisaged and initiated by Henry VIII endeavoured to retain the conception of a Catholic and Episcopal church and in this was far from the thoughts and aims of Calvin. But Calvinist ideas influenced the individual reformers, and traces of them can be discerned in Archbishop Cranmer's incomparable Prayer Book, which came into general use only after the death of Henry. Cranmer's Church was furnished with a Bible (the Wyclif Bible) that made God's words accessible to the people. And the

Calvinist faction was already actively demanding that the Church be purged of popish superstitions and turned in a Presbyterian direction (i.e. in the direction of a church in which priests are not subject to the overarching authority of a bishop). The ascent of Mary Tudor to the throne saw the enforced return to Roman Catholic orthodoxy. Many of the reforming bishops and theologians went into exile, the most significant of them to Calvin's Geneva or to other places where the influence of Calvin was prominent. Returning to complete the work of Reform under Elizabeth I, these learned churchmen brought with them Calvin's conviction that the true (Invisible) Church had been confiscated by the Popes, and could be regained only by following the guidance of the New Testament. And the Anglican Church as we know it today should be seen not as a victory over Roman Catholicism so much as a victory over Calvinism, on behalf of a revised Catholic Communion, in which the Church has been returned to its apostolic source.

Prior to the accession of James VI of Scotland to the English throne as James I, England and Scotland were distinct countries, brought together by geography, language and commerce, but with their own legal, political and religious institutions, and frequently at war with each other. Even after James I's accession, it was a full century before the Act of Union in 1707, which joined England and Scotland into a single kingdom – though one with separate legal and religious institutions. The ideas of Calvin were brought to Scotland from France, which was then allied with Scotland against England; and they fell in Scotland on ground more fertile than they encountered south of the border.

The subsequent evolution of the Scottish churches lies outside the scope of this book. Suffice it to say that the efforts of the Church of England to remain true to the Apostolic Succession, and to remain under the government of bishops who owed their authority to an unbroken chain of consecration from St Peter, were not duplicated in Scotland. In the wake of the violent and doctrinaire campaigns of the Calvinist John Knox (1514–72), Scotland found itself torn between a majority Presbyterian Church, consisting of independently governed Kirks that were frequently at loggerheads, and an Episcopalian minority that remained in communion with the Church of England. It was from the Episcopal Church of Scotland that the American Anglican Communion was to grow, since the Scottish bishops were not required to acknowledge the English sovereign as Head of their Church, and could, therefore, consecrate the bishops in America, where such an acknowledgement would be treason to the Constitution. To put the matter simply, the Church of England emerged from the Reformation and the many conflicts that it involved as a territorial church, centred on England, intimately bound up with the English language, English law and the political institutions of the English Crown, but in communion with other churches that shared one or more of its distinguishing features: language, and the liturgy shaped from it; the Episcopalian tradition; and the connection, whether direct or oblique, with the Crown of England.

Like the Roman Catholic Church and the Nonconformist churches, the reformed Church of England was, and is, a conciliar church in the spirit of Nicaea. Like the Church whose bishops met at Nicaea, it is integrally dependent upon the secular power. It is governed by statutes issued by Parliament, though usually on the advice of the bishops in Convocation. It is an established church, of which the sovereign is 'supreme governor', retaining the right to appoint bishops, which he or she does on the advice of the Prime Minister of the day, who could conceivably be an atheist, a Roman Catholic, a Muslim or a Jew. For three centuries it has been part of the inscrutable workings of British government, in which legislative, executive, judicial and religious authorities act independently but together, in order to maintain the ship of State on an even keel. But for all that, it is only one church among many that compete for the attention of the English people. Its status and powers were settled only at the Glorious Revolution of 1688, and it was promptly subjected to the Toleration Act of 1689, which told the Anglican Church that it was not, after all, *the* Church of England, but must tolerate the existence of a comet-tail of hangers-on.

The Toleration Act notwithstanding, membership of the Nonconformist churches for a while brought important disabilities. Nonconformists could not attend the ancient universities of Oxford and Cambridge or occupy a teaching position within them. And many of the professions remained closed throughout the eighteenth century to people who did not take the Anglican Communion. Nevertheless, the established character of our Church increasingly became a legal fiction. English law encouraged the growth of independent churches, just as it has encouraged other 'little platoons' of volunteers, to use the words of Burke. For, as well as recognizing the Roman-law concept of the corporation, English law has its own ingenious device of the trust, which enables a group of people to hold property for a purpose that is not the purpose of any one of them, and to administer that property for the common good.

The concept of the trust, which arose through the court of Chancery in the Middle Ages, has been described by F. W. Maitland as the greatest contribution of the English people to the development of jurisprudence.[15] It permits individuals to associate for a collective goal, for a charitable purpose, for educational or religious reasons, and to protect their common assets, regardless of whether they enjoy the status of a corporate person in law, and regardless of whether the State has granted to them any charter to authorize their dealings. It is a device that places in the hands of Everyman the ability to form durable institutions outside the control of the State. Trusts are governed by the branch of law known as 'equity', which applies principles of natural justice to dealings that may not have been explicitly regulated by the law. It has been used since the Middle Ages to protect civil associations from the encroachment of political power, and to safeguard the assets of charitable institutions. It is a striking example of the 'bottom up' jurisdiction associated with English common-law government, and expresses the deep-seated sense that people can create their own sources of legitimacy and do not need any authority other than conscience in order to find their way through the social labyrinth. Hence the networks of private schools, clubs, hospitals, almshouses, churches, teams, colleges and charities that grew in England during the seventeenth, eighteenth and nineteenth centuries.

By the time of the Glorious Revolution of 1688, therefore, it seemed that there could be no way of saving the pre-eminence of the Anglican Church even in England without recognizing it as one church among many – albeit a church associated with the workings of government, and led and protected by the Crown. It was in this form that the Church of England emerged from the tumult of the Civil Wars – a national church that claimed a kind of victory, while nervously conceding defeat. Although wound into the workings of government, like a beautiful fabric caught up in the wheels of a machine, it acknowledged the Presbyterian and Calvinist churches of Scotland, the Nonconformist churches and chapels of England and Wales, and even the sceptical Deists and Unitarians of the emerging Enlightenment, as having an equal claim to political protection. And gradually, as religious passions cooled, and people learned to appreciate this institution based in respect for the temporal order, the Anglican Church became a symbol of the English genius for compromise. It is in this light that we should see it, looking back over the conflicts from which our Church emerged, and over its subsequent peaceful reign as the spiritual representative of a people whose attitude to the Christian religion could be described as one of loyal indifference.

TWO

A National Church

In 1955 Philip Larkin published *The Less Deceived*, with its beautiful elegy entitled 'Church Going'. Its last stanza spoke to my generation of the experience that immediately greeted them on entering an English country church:

> A serious house on serious earth it is,
> In whose blent air all our compulsions meet,
> Are recognised, and robed as destinies.
> And that much never can be obsolete,
> Since someone will forever be surprising
> A hunger in himself to be more serious,
> And gravitating with it to this ground,
> Which, he once heard, was proper to grow wise in,
> If only that so many dead lie round.

On first reading, those are the thoughts of an archaeologist – the uncommitted visitor, unearthing the trinkets of a vanished piety. On second reading, however, you recognize that the lines don't merely describe the Anglican faith; they *express* it. Just *this* is what English people of my generation believed.

English churches tell of a people who for several centuries have preferred seriousness to doctrine, and routine to enthusiasm — people who hope for immortality but do not really expect it, except as a piece of English earth. The walls are covered with discreet memorials, placing the dead at the same convenient distance that they occupied when living. The pews are hard, uncomfortable, designed not for lingering and listening but for moments of penitence and doubt. The architecture is noble but bare and quiet, without the lofty aspiration of the French Gothic, or the devotional intimacy of an Italian chapel. More prominent than the altar are the lectern, the pulpit, the choir stalls and the organ. For this is a place of singing and speaking, in which Biblical English passes the lips of people who believe that holy thoughts need holy words, words somehow removed from the business of the world, like gems lifted from a jewel box and then quickly returned to the dark.

Christianity inherited from Judaism a hatred of idolatry, and from Greek polytheism a love of idols. Each Christian sect has had to resolve this paradox in its own way; the Anglican way being a compromise between the Calvinist and the Episcopal conceptions of the holy life, the one emphasizing doctrine and Biblical authority, the other emphasizing inscrutable sacraments and venerable traditions. The English Church recognized that, in the last analysis, God is not straightforwardly distinct from the way of representing him, even though identical with no physical thing. The earthly phenomenon through which he can be most accurately viewed is language – which has both a temporal reality and a timeless sense.

It is through language, therefore, that the Anglican Church has defined its God. It has drawn on the full resources of English to present a God who is dignified yet down-to-earth, at home in the world yet inscrutably withheld from it. God, as represented in the traditional services of the Anglican Church, is an Englishman, uncomfortable in the presence of enthusiasm, reluctant to make a fuss, but trapped into making public speeches. Like his fellow countrymen, God hides his discomfiture behind a solemn screen of words, using old-fashioned idioms that somehow excuse the severity of what he is bound by his office to say. In his presence you use the same antique language, and, although both of you know that this is in some measure a pretence, it suits you to rehearse your relationship in words that distance it from the world outside. More than in any country I have visited, the English country church of my youth was a home – God's house, the private space that is both here and elsewhere, a part of England, and an immortal projection of England in a realm beyond space and time.[16]

That was why the village churches of England have always made such a deep impression on those who enter them. God has been in residence here, among much-polished things, has moved with stiff English decorum around these light-filled spaces, has played the part of host to generations of people whose shyness he has respected and shared. You came away with a sense that time and eternity meet in this place today as they have always met and that both have a human face.

That this had not come about without a painful history is

evident from the very appearance of those quiet interiors. Iconoclasm and Puritan vandalism have swept through these arches like
a boiling tide through seashore caverns, and, retreating, have
left them bare. But you sense too that the storms have passed, that
the architecture is the purer and the cleaner for the brutal torrent
that has washed away its ornaments, and that the stunned tranquillity of those pitted walls will remain everlastingly. Compare the
village church with the nearest Methodist chapel and you will be
immediately struck by a difference in atmosphere that is something
more than atmosphere. The chapel has a pulpit, pews and a low
Communion table. But the architecture is plain – maybe brick,
wood or corrugated iron. The windows are sash windows of un-
stained glass, and the only aids to worship are Bibles and hymn
books. This is a place of sermons, in which everything is centred on
the pulpit and the word.

The Anglican church, by contrast, is a place of light and shade,
of tombs and recesses, of leaf mouldings and windows decked with
Gothic tracery and leaded glass. Strange aedicules line the chancel
walls – aumbry, sedilia and vestry door – suggesting the rituals of
an ancient temple. Choir stalls, rood screen, altar, font and pulpit are
as though dusted with holiness from the hands that carved them, and
the light that falls upon them is strangely intimate, seeming to come
from another source than the light that fills the nave. The scents of
damp stone and plaster, of altar flowers and dusty kneelers, mingle
to form a kind of restrained incense of their own, and you fall silent
as in the presence of a mystery. People travel up and down England
visiting these places, and there is one simple explanation as to why:

namely, because they are sacred. Thanks to the Anglican settlement, the *sacramental* character of our national church has survived from the time when the foundations of these shrines were laid to the moment when you step across their threshold out of a world that largely ignores them.

The churches and cathedrals of England are, for the most part, churches built by Roman Catholics, in the conviction that they will be monuments to an eternal Mother Church. But their identity with England has been settled beyond question by the history and culture of our country. They are symbols of a pastoral England that we know from our poets, painters and composers and from brief glimpses caught from time to time through the chaos of modern life. Our war memorials are built in a style that derives from them, and when we invoke the sacred presence of our country it is in words hewn from the rock of the King James Bible and the Anglican liturgy. The church towers stand in our towns and villages like distillations of the buried dead. And should from time to time the peal of bells ring out from them, and that strange caricature of music pour across the countryside, haunting the woods and the fields, and echoing ghost-like in the distant farmsteads, we hear the sound as a call to remembrance. It is the unmistakeable voice of ages past that sounds also in the verse of Tennyson, in the prose of Thomas Hardy and in the music of Elgar – great artists whose faith in England endured long after they had lost their faith in God. But what are we particularly called upon to remember? What is it that really counts in the history of our Church, and which makes it so important to our national culture?

42

When Lanfranc was appointed Archbishop of Canterbury at the insistence of William the Conqueror, he set about bringing the English Church into line with Rome, imposing the Canon Law, and replacing English clergy with Normans wherever he could. The English Church was to be an orthodox and obedient subject of the Bishop of Rome, and the spiritual isolation of the Anglo-Saxon Church was to be overcome at the same time and by the same process that the English were to lose their Anglo-Saxon identity. But it did not happen. Just as England remained Saxon in its culture, retaining the English language, the common law and the rugged culture of Everyman, so did the English Church very soon revert to its old identity as the Church of England, rather than the Church *in* England that Lanfranc had wished to create. Throughout the medieval era England saw a running conflict between King and Pope, and the English Church, although the Pope was nominally in charge of it, would frequently side with the King.

There are many reasons for this conflict. But one of first importance is the English law, which is the product of secular courts imposing a territorial jurisdiction. The English common law has always been understood as the *law of the land*, the law that prevails within the sovereign territory of England, and which, as the jurist Henry de Bracton affirmed in the twelfth century, appoints the King who enforces it. Our common law is inimical to laws made outside the kingdom, and for purposes that may be in conflict with those of the Crown. And it upholds the interests of plaintiffs against their oppressors, by a system of appeals that have created the lasting precedents of Chancery. The attempt by Rome to impose a universal jurisdiction, granting protection to the clergy and removing them from the secular courts of justice, has therefore been resisted by English jurists and sovereigns from the earliest days of the Plantagenet Crown.

The clash of jurisdictions came to a head in the dispute between Henry II and Thomas à Becket, who as Archbishop of Canterbury was the highest representative of the Holy See in England. The immediate issue was the measure of Canon Law, which held that a priest or clerk of the Church could, on being charged with a crime, claim benefit of clergy, so as to be tried under Canon Law by an ecclesiastical court, thus escaping the far more severe penalties of the King's jurisdiction. As is well known, this conflict led to the murder of the Archbishop, to the King's subsequent spectacular penance, and to the annual pilgrimage to Canterbury celebrated in Chaucer's unsurpassed gallery of medieval portraits. What is less well known is that the King was victorious in this conflict. King and Archbishop had clashed over a Royal Statute, the Constitutions of Clarendon, 1164, whose purpose was to maintain the territorial integrity of the King's jurisdiction and to prevent 'criminous clerks' from escaping its provisions. Although in his penitence the King removed two clauses that ran counter to Canon Law, the main effect of the Constitutions remained, ensuring that the Church persisted in England as a *subject* institution, even if representing a universal spiritual authority.

Subsequently, in 1213, King John surrendered the kingdom to Pope Innocent III, and received it back in fief, a measure that the Pope promptly abused by conferring ecclesiastical offices on Italian clergymen. This was one cause of the antagonism of the nobles towards King John, whom they forced to sign Magna Carta in 1215. The Charter makes no mention of the liege-lordship of the Pope and refers to the Church as '*Ecclesia Anglicana*', thus laying national claim to an institution that previous charters had described merely as 'Holy Church'. By 1231 a secret combination of noblemen and priests existed, threatening abbeys and other foundations if they made payments to Rome. By 1240 Roman priests were being regularly persecuted, and the Cardinal Legate Otho was menaced by an insurrection of Oxford students. A century later Edward III repudiated Pope Clement VI's nominations to English livings, and effectively took charge of clerical appointments.

Despite this resentment towards Rome, medieval England was marked by the ardour of its faith, manifest in the wonderful buildings that it has bequeathed to us, as well as the writings of its philosophers and poets. One thing that stands out, however, is the emergence of a religious ideal of discipleship in which the parish priest, rather than the wealthy bishop, is seen as the true representative of the Church. The portrait of this priest is given to us by Chaucer, in the Poor Parson of *The Canterbury Tales*, and the portrait of his congregation by Langland in *Piers Plowman* – two great fourteenth-century celebrations of English life as it then was, which awaken us both to the completeness with which Christianity had penetrated the English soul, and also to the completeness with which the English soul had penetrated Christianity, to produce the unique spirit that was later to find expression in the Anglican liturgy.

There is a kind of modern Englishman for whom the Anglican

call to remembrance has the distinctive accent of Langland. For H. J. Massingham, whose book *The Tree of Life* expresses the heady mixture of rural nostalgia and Guild Socialism that flourished between the two world wars, *Piers Plowman* is the archetypal document of English Christianity. Langland's poem, Massingham suggests, belongs to a world 'of which the village commoners and the Craft Guilds were the pillars and arches, and the Cistercian brotherhood part of the vaulting'.[17] In *Piers Plowman*, 'the peasant Christ takes on a definitely Anglicized form... and "God speed the Plough" acquires a spiritual profundity... that goes beyond Bunyan's idea of the New Faith'.

Massingham, writing in the Second World War, is seeking to discover a buried England that can rightly summon her children to the nation's defence. But his vision is not merely need-driven and private. The Englishness of the English religion can be clearly perceived in Chaucer and Langland. The Holy Church of Piers Plowman was an institution deeply intertwined with the English settlement, marked by yeoman individualism, by respect for simple manners and plain speaking, and by the same industrious piety that created the Gothic window and the hammer-beam roof. Its claim to the landscape was older than that of the Norman Kings, and the division of England into parishes and dioceses was associated with forms of local government in which the Church spoke as much for the Saxon peasant as for the Norman lord.

At the same time the century of Chaucer and Langland saw a renewal of the conflict between Rome and the Crown. The conflict was resolved by two statutes of Edward III – the Statute of

Provisors, 1351, and the Statute of Praemunire, 1353 – which effectively gave the King, rather than the Pope, the right to make
appointments to the priesthood, and to regulate the secular affairs
of the Church. This was also the century of Wyclif (1328–84), the
Oxford theologian who shaped the proto-Reformation. Wyclif gave
his name to the first widely used translation of the Bible into English
– the Wyclif Bible – a translation from the Vulgate made by others,
but which he caused to be copied and which he propagated as best
he could.

Later, with the invention of printing, it became clear that
vernacular translations of sacred texts could undermine church
authority, since they enable congregations to compare how the
clergy are with how the Gospels say they ought to be. Even in
Wyclif's time the vernacular Bible was regarded as a threat; still
more of a threat were the doctrines that Wyclif preached at Oxford,
and notably his attack on the idea of transubstantiation, fundamental to the Roman Catholic understanding of the Eucharist.

This last point is of great importance in explaining the Anglican
settlement. As I argued in the first chapter, the Christian religion
is not simply a set of doctrines to be believed. Of equal importance
to the medieval mind were the sacraments, and the opportunity
provided by an organized church to take part in those sacraments, to
celebrate the important rites of passage of the community, and to re-
enact Christ's sacrifice. Not that the doctrines and the sacraments
can be clearly distinguished: the Eucharist is interpreted through the
Trinity, and the Trinity, in turn, through the Eucharist. Scholastic
philosophers applied to both doctrine and sacrament the ingenious

conceptual apparatus that they had derived from Aristotle, and came up with the conclusion that Holy Communion involves a transubstantiation of the bread and wine into the body and blood of Christ. For such, they believed, is implied in the words used by Jesus himself at the Last Supper, and such does justice to the mystery of Communion, in which the faithful are invited to the closest possible union with their God.

The doctrine of transubstantiation was upheld by St Thomas Aquinas, and was officially endorsed by the medieval Church, to be later reaffirmed as fundamental by the Council of Trent. But among the many who found themselves unable to make sense of it, Wyclif was perhaps the most articulate, arguing that the doctrine was neither intelligible in itself nor necessary to understanding the true meaning of the Eucharist, which is to be found in the 'Real Presence' of Christ. This real presence can be granted, Wyclif argued, without supposing that the bread *becomes* Christ, and without adopting the strange position of William of Ockham, who argued that the bread ceases to be a substance altogether. Hence the words of the Last Supper, 'This is my body', can be literally true, even though the bread that the Saviour refers to remains bread. For Christ can be present in something through its spiritual significance, just as he is present among us, as he promised, when we gather together in his name.

To modern people the debate over transubstantiation may appear quaint – a form of logical gymnastics, and a trading of absurdities. For Wyclif, however, the question was of the greatest urgency. The act of Communion is one of two sacraments associated with the life of Christ – the other being Baptism. It is clear from the Gospel narrative that the Saviour regarded these two sacraments as marking out the moral and metaphysical space of his Church. Through Baptism we enter the Church, and through Communion we renew our commitment, becoming 'members of Christ', as St Paul expressed it. For Wyclif, therefore, Communion should not remain a mystery, and his desire to explain it to the ordinary communicant was of a piece with his advocacy of the vernacular Bible. St Anselm of Canterbury had famously broached the topic of mystery in the remark *'credo ut intelligam'* – I believe in order to understand. Only through faith, itself a gift of God's grace, could a mere mortal be raised to the point of comprehending the divine plan, and seeing what was intended and achieved by Christ's sacrifice. Wyclif was one of many Englishmen of his time who were of the opposite persuasion, holding that the promises of Christianity should be understood in order to be believed. And this is the root of Protestant spirituality, the real reason not only for the use of the vernacular language, but also for eschewing any ritual or ceremony that is not necessary to explaining God's purpose. By understanding the Bible, Christians, according to the Protestant way of thinking, enter into a direct relation with their Saviour, and the Church exists not to clothe this fact in mystery but on the contrary to reveal it, and to implant it in the heart of the believer.

Later, partly under Calvinist influence, the belief in transubstantiation was to become a kind of test, whereby a lingering attachment to Rome could be discerned in people who had outwardly accepted the Reformation. Elizabethan divines singled out this doctrine as chief among the obfuscations with which the Popes had poisoned the pure message of the Gospels. It was again emphasized by the seventeenth-century Test Acts, designed to weed out 'popery' from the emerging national church, and as late as 1704, in the reign of Queen Anne, an Oath of Conformity was introduced by 'an act to prevent the further growth of popery', requiring all who aspired to any kind of official office to testify 'solemnly and sincerely, in the presence of God' that they believe 'that in the sacrament of the Lord's Supper there is not any transubstantiation of the elements of bread and wine into the body and blood of Christ, at or after the consecration thereof by any person whatever'. The Thirty-nine Articles that define the official creed of the Church of England still contain, in Article 28, the following warning:

> Transubstantiation (or the change of the substance of Bread and Wine) in the Supper of the Lord, cannot be proved by Holy Writ; but is repugnant to the plain words of Scripture, overthroweth the nature of a Sacrament, and hath given occasion to many superstitions.

The revulsion that the doctrine aroused among the Elizabethan divines derived not from any rejection of sacraments but, on the contrary, from a desire to retain them – to establish a sacramental church that honestly explained itself to its members. This, in a nutshell, was the Anglican mission, and it began with Wyclif, long before the Reformation had turned the order of Christendom upside down.

Forms of Protestantism were to emerge that reject Holy Communion altogether, or downgrade it to a mere commemoration of the Last Supper, with no metaphysical significance. But the Anglican Church as we know it resulted from a struggle to retain Holy Communion, and to retain the sacrificial altar in the central place that it had always occupied, as a symbol of the gifts that come from God and which are also offered up to him. Our Church was to be an institution shaped by the needs and aspirations of a secular and political community, in which the primal blood sacrifice of the Saviour was nevertheless constantly celebrated – a place in human history, which would be outside space and time. Hence Article 28 goes on to explain that 'the Body of Christ is given, taken, and eaten, in the Supper, only after an heavenly and spiritual manner. And the mean whereby the Body of Christ is received and eaten in the Supper is Faith.'

In the age of Victorian scepticism, it was possible to look back on the controversy over the Eucharist as a striking illustration of what Victorian rationalists considered to be the impenetrable mystery that lies at the heart of the religious urge, and which seems to require people to regard as matters of life and death precisely those doctrines that make least sense to the enquiring mind, and which can perhaps never be explained to the satisfaction either of those who believe them or of those who doubt. Thus we find Macaulay writing, in his 1840 essay on Ranke's *History of the Popes*:

when we reflect that Sir Thomas More was ready to die for the doctrine of transubstantiation, we cannot but feel some doubt whether the doctrine of transubstantiation may not triumph over all opposition. More was a man of eminent talents. He had all the information on the subject that we have, or that, while the world lasts, any human being will have. The text, 'This is my body', was in his New Testament as it is in ours. The absurdity of the literal interpretation was as great and obvious in the sixteenth century as it is now. No progress that science has made, or will make, can add to what seems to us the overwhelming force of the argument against the Real Presence. We are, therefore, unable to understand why what Sir Thomas More believed respecting transubstantiation may not be believed to the end of time by men equal in abilities and honesty to Sir Thomas More...[18]

Macaulay there confuses the doctrine of transubstantiation with that of the Real Presence. But that only reinforces his point: the attempts by Wyclif and the Anglican divines to distinguish the indistinguishable show that in religion we feel most strongly about the things that cannot be explained, and pit mystery against mystery in passionate advocacy, precisely because we do not know what hangs on victory other than the vindication of *my* church against *yours*. In the long run it has been the strength of the Anglican Church that it has both understood this point, and at the same time helped us to live in retreat from it. Ours is a *settled* church, in which doctrinal differences have been marginalized, and custom, ceremony and unthreatening mysteries placed in the foreground. Anglican doctrine is not sharpened by Biblical exegesis and argumentative commentary, such as that provided by Calvin in his line-by-line exposition of the Gospels. It is softened through ceremony, and buried in the folds of a ritual cloak so that only its outlines appear.

Of course, it was not like that in Wyclif's day, and his theological heresies, his propagation of the vernacular Bible and his advocacy of a purified religious life led to the first stirrings of the conflict that was to release much of Europe from the grip of Rome. In Wyclif's lifetime the Roman Church had suffered a great blow to its authority, with the schism that saw two rival Popes on the throne of St Peter, one in Rome, the other in Avignon, both contending with every kind of secular weapon for absolute authority over the kings and princes of Europe. And for a while it seemed that disaffection with a church that had lost its definite article would spread. The religious orders, which had had such a profound effect on the shaping of medieval society, began rapidly to decline, and religious observance lost some of its day-to-day character. However, Wyclif's followers (the Lollards, so called from their alleged habit of mumbling) never succeeded in creating an organized alternative to the Roman Catholic Communion, and their brief rebellion was aborted in 1415 with the execution of their leader, Sir John Oldcastle. After that, although Wyclif's influence remained among the reforming priesthood, the Church in England returned to established customs.[19] Wyclif himself was tried on several occasions, and survived largely thanks to his patron, the powerful John of Gaunt, who was also patron, and briefly brother-in-law, of Chaucer. Even so, Wyclif was dismissed from his Chair at Oxford and died in

relative obscurity as a country parson. Only later, with the first stirrings of the Reformation in the writing and preaching of Jan Hus
in Prague, did Wyclif's thinking play a decisive role. The Roman
Church was by then on the defensive, and Hus, summoned to the
Council of Constance, was burned there at the stake, a grant of safe
passage notwithstanding.

At the root of every religion is a revelation – a call to membership, which promises release from worldly impurities and from the
fear of death, in return for adherence to certain doctrines and strict
compliance to a community-forming code. Hence religions mark
out the rites of passage through which individuals affirm their social
membership. And because people are constantly straying from the
beaten path, constantly arming themselves against each other, constantly frothing up in envy and resentment and seeking a dominion
that the community denies, religions also offer purifying rituals,
conferring spiritual renewal and social peace.

In the case of Christianity the central ritual is a sacrifice – the
sacrifice of God himself, who showed us how to renounce the world
and to suffer the worst that men can do to us while at the same time
focusing our moral energies on the work of forgiveness. Christ's
sacrifice is rehearsed in the Eucharist, and it is clear that its meaning
transcends anything that could be summarized in a piece of cobbled
metaphysics of the kind offered by Ockham or Wyclif. And that is
why so many of the disputes that occurred in the wake of the
Reformation concerned the nature of the Eucharist – for they were
disputes as to who was entitled to claim the benefit of this sacrifice,
who was *really* called to discipleship, and therefore who could claim

membership of the community of the saved. This is not to say that doctrinal disputes were merely empty, but rather to point out that what was at stake in them was always something deeper than doctrine – not only the faith and hope of the individual believer, but the identity of a community, whose cohesion was wrapped up in a shared enactment of a common faith.

For that very reason it has never been easy for a political community either to ignore the religious beliefs of its members, or to organize the laws and conventions of government without reference to them. The separate allegiance to Caesar and to God that Christ made fundamental to his Church is easier to describe than to maintain, and one way of understanding the Reformation is as a temporary coalescence of the two jurisdictions, under the growing pressure of national sentiment and territorial claims. Boundaries once settled by dynastic agreements were now marked by language, custom and jurisdiction. The Holy Roman Empire had ceased, in the eyes of most ordinary Europeans, to be either holy, or Roman or an empire, and Henry VIII's claim that England is 'an empire, entire unto itself' was simply the natural expression of an emerging sense of nationhood, and of the primacy of secular law and vernacular language in defining the obedience of the subject.

The call for a vernacular Bible was, therefore, not simply an appeal for an intelligible text. It was also an expression of communal sentiment on the part of people united as much by language as by faith. The defiance of Rome was more a rejection of foreign domination and foreign appointments to the priesthood than a call for a new interpretation of the Gospels. Henry VIII was awarded the title of *Fidei Defensor* – defender of the faith – by Pope Leo X, for his defence of the Church against the calumnies of Luther, a defence composed with the help of Henry's Lord Chancellor, Sir Thomas More, whom Henry subsequently martyred. Henry's break with Rome was a dynastic rather than a dogmatic decision: he needed a male heir, and his wife, Catherine of Aragon (who was also *Fidei Defensor* in her own right), could not produce one. The refusal of the Pope to grant an annulment of Henry's first marriage was experienced by the King as a threat to his sovereignty. In declaring himself Head of the Church Henry hoped to end the possibility of a King being controlled from outside the kingdom in an affair of state such as this one, concerning the succession to the Crown. In doing so he was bound to unleash nationalist sentiment, and also to create an opportunity for a renewed attempt to create a reformed Church in England – perhaps even a reformed Church *of* England.

It should be said, however, that Henry's decision to declare himself Head of the Church in England merely brought to completion the long-standing separatist tendency of the English Crown and the English people. The Act of Supremacy, passed by Parliament in 1534, opened the way to the Reformation, but was not in itself designed as a reform of the Church. It was rather a petulant gesture directed at the Holy See, and a declaration of a new kind of sovereignty – the sovereignty that we associate with the nation state. It followed the Act in Restraint of Appeals to Rome, 1533, drafted by Henry's confidential minister, Thomas Cromwell, a strong Protestant who was to be granted the title 'high vicar of spirituality under the King' in 1536, and who oversaw the destruction of the monasteries, before being himself destroyed by Henry. The Act of 1533 outlawed appeals to Rome on ecclesiastical matters, and declared that:

> this realm of England is an Empire, and so hath been accepted in the world, governed by one Supreme Head and King having the dignity and royal estate of the Imperial Crown of the same, unto whom a body politic compact of all sorts and degrees of people divided in terms and by names of Spirituality and Temporality, be bounden and owe to bear next to God a natural and humble obedience.

Historians have in general followed Sir Geoffrey Elton[20] in seeing this as a declaration of national self-sufficiency, requiring that all sources of authority in the new political order must be *internal to the kingdom*.

It is well beyond the scope of this short book to describe what followed. Suffice it to say that, while the English Church was divided over the matter of Henry's divorce, the matter was resolved when the incumbent at Canterbury, Archbishop Warham, died, leaving Henry free to appoint Thomas Cranmer (1489–1556) as his successor. Cranmer had been a member of the commission appointed to negotiate the dissolution of Henry's first marriage, and was himself no stranger to the reproductive urge, being twice married, even though bound by undertakings of celibacy both to the Church and to the Cambridge college (Jesus) of which he was a Fellow. He acknowledged his surviving wife and children only after the death of Henry, when he judged it safe to do so, as the Archbishop of a church that no longer regarded either Holy Orders or Matrimony as sacraments.

In the long run the issue of celibacy was to be central to the tension between the Roman Catholic and the Anglican Churches. But of more pressing concern to Cranmer was the liturgy, which he wished to bring within reach of the people, combining clear doctrine with sacramental language in a way that would ensure the continuity of an Episcopal church. His strong support for the use of the vernacular in the liturgy led to his being appointed to draft an English litany for the Mass. His words are still in use in the services of the Anglican Church, immortalizing the conflict that gave rise to them, by placing the reigning sovereign in the centre of the liturgical drama, in prayers that inevitably strike the modern churchgoer as quaint.

By the time of Cranmer's litany the effects of the Reformation were being felt everywhere in the British Isles. The appearance of a new translation of the Bible by William Tyndale, and the introduction of printing presses and cheap paper, soon made the Bible into a universal object of study among the literate. Tyndale was executed in Bruges (where he had sought refuge) in 1536, at Henry VIII's request, since he had been an articulate and vehement opponent of the King's divorce. But it was the same King Henry who authorized the issuing of the English Bibles, all based on Tyndale's translation, four years later. That episode typifies all that was to occur in the reign of Henry – orders made and countermanded, assaults on the Papacy followed by fervent protestations of Catholic orthodoxy, wrestling with the clergy matched by pious submission to their advice, much of it following the curious logic of Henry's hormones, and all of it animated by the one dominant concern, which was to assert the supremacy of the Crown over every rival source of authority in the Kingdom of England and Wales.

The rebuke to Luther that had earned King Henry the title of *Fidei Defensor* was 'A Defence of the Seven Sacraments'. It upheld the traditional seven sacraments through which the Church maintained its ritual presence in the lives of the faithful. Luther's doctrine of 'justification by faith alone' encouraged Christians to bypass the 'justification by works' through which the Church administered its indulgences. Luther acknowledged only three sacraments – Baptism, Eucharist and Penance (one more than Calvin) – thereby substantially curtailing the presence of the Church in the lives of its members. Matrimony and Holy Orders, having lost their sacramental status, were no longer to be thought of as unbreakable vows before God, but as human institutions that could both receive and also lose the Almighty's blessing. Not surprisingly these ideas caused moral and spiritual havoc once released into the air of Henry's England, and it was one purpose of Archbishop Cranmer to retain what he could of the sacramental inheritance of the Church, while accommodating the new Protestant spirit, for which faith, doctrine and God's Word took precedence over the old rituals and ceremonies. The result was the Book of Common Prayer, issued in 1549, during the reign of Henry's frail son Edward VI.

It is a measure of Henry's reluctance to break completely with the Catholic tradition that services had remained in Latin

throughout his reign. While proceeding against the Church whenever there was a financial or political gain from doing so, he never
wished to deny its special place in his subjects' lives, or its unique
claims to their devotion. Even the Dissolution of the Monasteries,
perhaps the cruellest and least popular of the anti-Roman measures
of Henry's reign, was more the work of Thomas Cromwell than
of Henry himself. If the King supported the measure, it was from
financial rather than religious motives. And if he incurred blame for
it, this was as much for his failure to put anything in the place of the
social and educational services that the monasteries had provided, as
for the act of sacrilege in forcibly releasing religious people from
their vows.[21] The brief reign of Edward VI saw, however, a rapid
expansion of the Protestant movement, with officially sanctioned
iconoclasm, the abolition of surplices and liturgical plate, even the
replacement of the stone altar with a simple wooden Communion
table from behind which the priest would administer the sacrament,
facing the congregation. Images, plate, stained glass and sculpted
stone were damaged or destroyed, and the churches of England
suffered the first of the great surges of vandalism that were to leave
them, by the end of the seventeenth century, largely bare of ornament.

The conflict over images and symbols was not simply between
reformers and Papal loyalists. It was also a conflict internal to the
new Anglican Church, which from the very beginning existed in
'high church' and 'low church' versions, the first striving to retain
what it could of the ceremonial drama of the Roman liturgy, the
second aiming to create a new 'meeting house' image of Christian

worship. The conflict was already heating up in the days of Queen Elizabeth I, with the word 'puritan' being used for the first time in 1564, to describe those who objected to the 'ornaments' rubric of the Elizabethan Prayer Book and who rebelled against the Queen's desire to impose uniformity. The Puritans were strongly Calvinist in tendency, and fired up by an English Bible issued in Geneva in 1560 (the 'Geneva Bible'), which was embellished with politically charged and sometimes incendiary marginalia. They leaned towards a Presbyterian conception of the Church, and loudly criticized the 'childish and superstitious toyes' (as their leader Thomas Cartwright put it) that the English Church had retained, including Eucharistic vestments, the sign of the cross at Baptism, the ring of marriage and bowing at the name of Jesus.

In *A Treatise of Reformation without Tarrying for Any* (1582) Robert Browne took up the cause, urging his readers to 'refuse all ungodly communion with wicked persons'. The denunciations of trumpery and priestcraft were to be heard more loudly in the seventeenth century, when the low church Protestants broke away to form churches of their own. Meanwhile, Richard Hooker (1554–1600), in the greatest work of Anglican theology that we possess, gently rebuked the Puritans for preferring accident to essence in the matter of faith. For Hooker the Puritans were objecting to harmless practices that conflict with no real item of Christian belief. These practices have the authority of tradition, violate no natural law of reason, and bring comfort to ordinary believers. Hooker's *Laws of Ecclesiastical Polity* remains the most subtle existing defence of an 'established' church – a church that, while remaining obedient to its apostolic mission, strives to uphold the secular jurisdiction and to co-operate in maintaining civil order. Hooker clearly understood both the community-forming and the community-destroying tendencies of religion, and the nature of a church, as an institution-alization of both. Hence he recognized that any church must have two dominant duties: to *inspire* religious sentiment, and also to *contain* it.

Many would say that the Anglican Church has succeeded so well in the second of those duties as to extinguish the first, proving itself incapable of retaining either John Wesley or John Henry Newman, the two most passionate vessels of the Christian faith that it has produced in modern times, the one low church and the other high church. Suffice it to say that we should not be surprised if to this day there exist both an evangelical extreme of our Church, in which preaching is the dominant mode of address, and an 'Anglo-Catholic' extreme that closely follows the Tridentine liturgy of the Mass, with the priest facing the altar at the end of the church, wearing ornate vestments and distributing unleavened bread to the communicants. It is one part of the genius of Anglicanism that it has been able to retain Anglo-Catholics and Evangelicals within a single 'broad church', as Coleridge described it. How this came about is one part of the extraordinary history of seventeenth-century England. What it means for us today is a subject to which I return in later chapters.

Happily, Cranmer's Prayer Book (an adaptation of the Old Sarum Rite, and probably the work of several hands) won the approval of the King and his counsellors. A revised version, the 1552 Book of Common Prayer, was imposed (to the anger of the Puritans) throughout the land, and a further revision was adopted in 1662. That book, combined with the Authorized Version of the Bible, has formed the heart of the Anglican faith, from the settlement of 1688 to the present day. Between 1552 and 1662, however, the religious life of England was in a fever of dissent and reaction. The attempt by Mary Tudor to reimpose Catholic orthodoxy was not only a failure in itself. It drove the most important of the Anglican divines into exile, large numbers to Geneva or other places where they absorbed the doctrines of John Calvin. When Mary was succeeded by Elizabeth, and the Act of Supremacy, which had been repealed in 1554, was again imposed in 1558, the Church of England began to suffer from the strong internal conflict mentioned above, between the Presbyterian Puritans, and the Episcopal Catholics.

Various attempts had been made under Henry VIII and Edward VI to produce a compendium of Anglican doctrine, with strong inputs from both German Lutherans, advocating the Confession of Augsburg, and Calvinists from France and Switzerland, arguing for Presbyterianism and the doctrines of predestination and prevenient Grace. These early attempts at defining a church that was to be Apostolic, Episcopal, Protestant and in some way under the jurisdiction of the Crown culminated in forty-two Articles of Anglican belief prepared by Cranmer and issued by Royal Mandate in 1553. These Articles were never enforced, on account of the accession of Mary to the throne. But a Convocation of the Church under Archbishop Matthew Parker in 1563 reworked Cranmer's material in the form of the Thirty-nine Articles, removing the more extreme Calvinist elements, and establishing a compromise that, it was hoped, would extend the protection of the Church to all true Christians in the land, while defining the Church of England as an Episcopal and Apostolic church, against the competing claims of Rome on the one hand, and the Calvinist, Presbyterian and Anabaptist dissenters on the other. These Articles and the Book of Common Prayer define the doctrine and the practice of the Anglican Church, and remain valid to this day, though how many who now call themselves Anglican either believe the Articles or know what they are must surely be doubted.

The century of conflict that followed is one about which there will never be agreement either among historians or among those who look back to those times for the root of their religious or political allegiance. The Act of Supremacy critically implicated the Crown, and therefore the political order, in the religious turmoil of England. But it also made that religious turmoil into a political matter, one that could be the subject of Parliamentary discussion and legislative decisions in which the whole kingdom was involved. Hence during the reign of Elizabeth there emerged a new kind of theologian, one actively involved in the affairs of both Church and State, whose principal endeavour was to reconcile the competing factions within the new Protestant Church. Bishop Jewel's *Apology for the Church of England*, first published in Latin in 1562, was directed primarily against those who leaned towards Rome. Jewel had begun his ministry as a Calvin-influenced Puritan, and his work (translated into English by Anne Bacon, mother of the philosopher) helped to persuade Calvinists that they could accept the Episcopal dispensation of the English Church.

More significant than Jewel, however, was his protégé, the saintly Richard Hooker, whose unfinished *Laws of Ecclesiastical Polity* addressed the whole question of the status of the Church in the new dispensation. The crucial issue that, for Hooker, was both definitive of the Christian faith, and the main point of contention between the English Church and the Church of Rome, was the issue of the Incarnation. Hooker had a certain respect for Calvinism, but sought to defend the sacramental conception of the Church, arguing that Christians cannot hope to be snatched to salvation, but must 'grow in grace', through participating in the divine life that was brought to us through the Incarnation. The sacraments are not simply an ornament of faith, which could be dispensed with by those who had rectified their standing in the eyes of God. They are of the essence of a church, the sign and continuation of the Incarnation. They bound the Church of England to the Body of Christ, and their status could not be undermined simply because the Roman Church also adhered to them.

Thanks in part to Hooker's influence, the Church that emerged from Elizabeth's reign was an ecumenical one, not a synthesis of rival views, but a panoply spread over all those Christian obediences that could honestly accept the Act of Supremacy and the Episcopal government. It was a Protestant Church in conscious rebellion against Rome and the Papacy. It accepted a married priesthood, permitted divorce (in certain circumstances), and contained many iconoclastic and Puritan elements. It rejected the cult of saints and the Virgin Mary, leaving a hole in the hearts of many English people that was only partly filled by their adoration for the Virgin Queen.

But it was an Episcopal church, which maintained ceremonial traditions, and embraced the deepest paradox of Christianity, namely the sacrament in which God himself is sacrificed. Lancelot Andrewes, the greatest divine of the age immediately following that of Hooker, put the point thus, that Christ is 'A sacrifice—so, to be slain; a propitiatory sacrifice—so, to be eaten.'[22] The significance of those words will emerge in later chapters. Suffice it to say that they are not innocent words, and that they committed the Church of England to doctrines and practices that the Puritans and the Calvinists accepted only with difficulty, and which others found hard to distinguish from the Papal alternative. Nevertheless, the effect of the Elizabethan settlement was to create a church that had the broad endorsement of the nation, and a nation that had the broad endorsement of the Church.

It is possible to understand the Civil Wars, the execution of King Charles I, the Long Parliament and the Interregnum as the outcome of secular forces and 'class struggles'. But this does not alter the fact that almost all the public quarrels before, during and immediately after the Civil Wars were in some degree about religion, and took their inspiration and their slogans from the new translation of the Bible, authorized by King James I.[23] The most heated of the Parliamentary debates concern ecclesiastical reform and the rights of separatists and dissenters. The accession of James I to the Crown had brought the Calvinist and Presbyterian Church of Scotland into the picture – a church that neither agreed to receive the King as its head nor agreed to receive anyone else. James VI of Scotland, before becoming King of England, had attempted to install Episcopal governance in the Church of Scotland, and Charles I had imposed the Book of Common Prayer – a move that led to rioting, followed by the 'Bishops' Wars', in which the Calvinists and Puritans of Scotland anticipated the Civil Wars that were soon to ravage England. Subsequently, the Long Parliament, in order to enlist the support of the Scots against the Royalist armies, entered into a 'Solemn League and Covenant' with the Scottish Covenantors. This stopped short of promising a Presbyterian church in England, but nevertheless undertook to complete the Reformation in both England and Ireland in a manner agreeable to the Scottish churches.

During the Civil Wars the fervent Calvinism of the Scottish reformer John Knox found many supporters in Parliament, as did churches, fellowships and troublemakers eager to announce the Second Coming – notably the Fifth Monarchy Men and the so-called Ranters. Chiliasm (the belief in the Millennium prophesied in the Book of Revelation) has a long history in Christian eschatology, and its medieval upsurges were frequently traumatic, even if locally confined. Its role in the civil turmoil of seventeenth-century England was critical, endowing every faction with an incendiary mixture of real courage and false hopes, as one after another the contending sects took up arms in a fight for 'Godly rule'.

A sceptical spirit, looking back at the religious enthusiasms of the English seventeenth century, would surely be tempted to conclude that the Roman Catholic Church was right to insist that the Holy Book should be filtered through the cloth of priestly Latin, and fed only in small doses to the people. For there is no doubt that the Book of Revelation was as poisonous in seventeenth-century England as *The Communist Manifesto* was in nineteenth-century Russia. Like *The Communist Manifesto*, it both prophesies the imminent future, and exhorts its readers to work for it – a peculiarly toxic combination that recruits both resentment and desire, and forges from their union an implacable hatred of the ordinary world of peaceful compromise. By invoking the 'New Jerusalem' that will arise inexorably when the reign of the 'Whore of Babylon' has at last been extinguished, the Book of Revelation implants the unforgettable imagery of a bloodthirsty schizophrenic straight into the amygdala of the puritanical believer. And its message, translated into contemporary terms by Calvin's Commentaries and by the marginal notes in the Geneva Bible, was an incitement to violence against the Roman Catholics and any who remotely sympathized with them.

Unprotected by a ceremonial church and a mystery-mongering priesthood, drunk on the blood of recent martyrs, and sensing all about him the presence of the Whore, the new type of Christian zealot was in a life-and-death struggle with the Prince of Darkness, and understood every compromise as a defeat. The Pope ceased to be a mortal being and became Antichrist, and the Roman Church's claim to be the vessel of the Holy Spirit was upheld in the negative. This sense of living in ultimate confrontation with the enemy of mankind is a wonderfully pliable and object-hungry feeling. Directed now at the Church of Rome it can as easily veer towards its Anglican successor, and even more easily towards the one in the next pew, who has mistakenly assumed that the Real Presence requires transubstantiation, or who has ill-advisedly bowed at the name of Jesus or in a forgetful moment made the sign of the cross. As the conflicts developed, any claim to traditional authority, to Episcopal privilege, or to a first-hand involvement in mysteries that are hidden from the purified eyes of the true believer would summon the 'Whore of Babylon' reflex, and with it the desire to smash, bind and murder in the name of the Lord. So the Puritan would strive 'to prove his doctrine orthodox / By apostolic blows and knocks', as the seventeenth-century poet Samuel Butler famously put it in *Hudibras* (1662–78), his satirical commentary on the events of the time.

If the Anglican Church was able to survive this madness it was partly due to Mary Tudor and her persecutions. For the cruelties of Mary's reign gave rise to the work of astute propaganda that linked the Anglican Church with the trials of the children of Israel and with the early martyrs of the Church. Foxe's *Book of Martyrs* (1563) created a claim of authority far stronger, in its way, than that of the Apostolic Succession, which is the claim of blood sacrifice – the very claim made in the words that I quoted from Bishop Andrewes. The book was as influential in the short term as any production of the reign of Elizabeth, and an interesting proof of the fact that the historical significance of ideas has little or no connection with their intellectual merit. A Convocation of Bishops in 1571 ordered that a copy of this book should be placed, together with the Bishop's Bible (the then accepted vernacular version of Holy Scripture), in every cathedral.

John Foxe's animated descriptions of the sufferings of Mary's victims are designed to show that the Reformation was continuous with the original revelation of God's purpose, and that the blood sacrifices of Mary Tudor's reign were the spiritual equivalent of those early martyrdoms through which Christianity first justified its claims. The Papal legions imposed death and suffering on those who bore witness against them: hence they were the very legions that had striven from the beginning to oppose the reign of Christ. There can be no compromise with Antichrist: such was the message passed on to the Protestant sects whose political representatives rampaged in Parliament on behalf of 'Godly rule' during the Civil Wars. But there was another message too: namely, that the Anglican Church had been first in the field, that it had established its credentials, and should not be taken as a target of the prevailing rage. In this way Foxe's book served to protect the Anglican Church from the worst of the hysteria that swept across our country during the seventeenth century. It did not prevent the Puritans from sacking the churches yet again, nor did it reconcile the Presbyterian faction to the idea that bishops too could be martyrs. But it made the Church of England into a part of the great chain of suffering, which was the true Apostolic Succession and one that was a spiritual rather than a worldly presence. Foxe's book was an apology for the great presumption of our Church in claiming the sovereign of England as its head. For it showed that this claim brought no protection, and that the spirit of the Church lay, as ever, in the sacrifice of those who had given their lives to it.

Foxe was also partly responsible for a new self-image of reformed Christianity – one shaped by a reading of the Old

Testament, and its story of a chosen people, striving constantly to escape its heathen enemies, and to reunite with its God. The image of English Protestants as the new children of Israel was appropriated both by Anglicans and by the separatist sects that warred against them. It was a vital element of the Puritan worldview, and was brought to America by the Pilgrim Fathers – separatists who had fled first to the Netherlands before undertaking the journey to Massachusetts. And throughout the conflicts of the seventeenth century the reforming sects of England clothed themselves in the Old Testament stories, claiming the rights and duties of a chosen people fighting for the New Jerusalem against the reign of the Whore. The link then forged between England and the Holy City entered into the national culture, to receive its greatest expression over a century later in the poetry of William Blake.

The strife of the seventeenth century gave rise to works of literature every bit as great as the best of Blake, including one popular masterpiece that will never be equalled for its religious simplicity and its capacity to engage the imagination of Everyman: *The Pilgrim's Progress* (1678) by the Puritan John Bunyan (1628–88), conceived when the author was held in prison for preaching without the authority of the Church. It also gave rise to the greatest work of political philosophy that the English have produced, and to the only epic poem in English that approaches those of Homer and Virgil. But no two works can be further from each other in intent than these last two: the *Leviathan* of Hobbes (1651) and Milton's *Paradise Lost* (1667). Each stands at the intellectual summit of the two warring mounds of the century-long contest.

Milton (1608–74) was an urbane and much travelled observer of the world, a lover of Italian literature and Mediterranean culture who ought, by rights, to have been a Cavalier. In fact, he was an official in Cromwell's government, a republican, and a dissenting Christian who saw political order and religious belief as affairs between the individual and God and who, in later life, attended no form of public worship. Hobbes (1588–1679), the son of a poor country parson, who emerged from obscurity by a series of lucky accidents, ought by rights to have been a Roundhead. In fact, he was a Royalist fugitive and an agnostic, who regarded obedience to Caesar as the *sine qua non* of social life, and religion as a matter to be settled to the convenience of government and in the interest of peace. For all their differences, Milton and Hobbes had one thing in common: they had both looked into the abyss, and seen that destruction is natural to man, and religion not a cure for it but simply one of its many occasions.

Milton's incomparable descriptions of sexual love, of the proud and defiant Satan, and of the fragile order of paradise, so easily overthrown, are ostensibly Christian, but also foundationless. Envy, ambition, desire and jealousy are seen as eternal forces that break through every order designed to contain them. There is no resolution, and although Christ's redeeming mission is foretold in the poem, we know that he will root out the primeval resentment only by falling victim to it. The Cosmos, as Milton describes it, is shot through with a fatal flaw, which is freedom. And yet freedom is also the highest good. Satan cannot be what God intended in creating the dominions, princedoms and powers without the gift of freedom, and one aspect of freedom is the desire for a dominion of one's own. Adam and Eve could not be the cherished goal of the divine plan if they were not also free to disobey, and with unrivalled penetration Milton shows that human love is a realization of our nature as reasoning and choosing creatures, so that love too can go wrong.

The same emphasis on freedom can be found in Milton's political works – in his defence of divorce, his attack on censorship, and his *Eikonoklastes*, directed against the contemporary cult of King Charles the Martyr. In the words of Mark Pattison,

> He defended religious liberty against the Prelates, civil liberty against the Crown, the liberty of the press against the executive, liberty of conscience against the Presbyterians, and domestic liberty against the tyranny of canon law. Milton's pamphlets might have been stamped with the motto which Selden inscribed in Greek in all his books, "Liberty before everything".[24]

Milton's is a world cast loose from all man-made authority, in which human beings are face to face with their freedom to choose, and baffled by it. Only in the pure, unmediated confrontation with God, in prayer and meditation, is the human need for guidance supplied.

Paradise Lost, *Paradise Regained* and *Samson Agonistes* retold the legends of the Torah as English legends; and Milton's Latinate diction, acting on minds already shaped by the King James Bible and the Prayer Book, showed that English can match Hebrew, Greek and Latin as a voice of the Christian revelation. This revelation could be interpreted afresh by new generations of English people, but it had an unassailable authority on account of the language that had been shaped to contain it. The Anglican Church emerged into the light of modernity with the same treasure that Muhammad carried back to Mecca from his Medina exile – a revelation and a language that had been fused together, so that the revelation was spoken into the heart of the believer and had become the voice of God.

Bunyan and Milton show two sides of English Christianity – the one a fervent believer in the Gospel message of sin and redemption, refracted through the severe lens of seventeenth-century Puritanism, the other a sophisticated cosmopolitan poet, aware of the insoluble metaphysical conundrums to which faith in all its forms gives rise, and anxious above all to impress on his readers the uniqueness of the human soul in the work of creation. Between them Bunyan and Milton define a religious sensibility that endured as the spiritual resource of the English until the days of my own youth.

But Anglicanism achieved a synthesis of which that sensibility was only a part. Equally important has been the sceptical retreat from enthusiasm that found expression in the work of Thomas Hobbes. For Hobbes nothing was more important than civil peace, and civil peace was not the natural gift of religion. On the contrary, religion was one of the chief dangers, a force that must be contained within an established church, obedient to the civil power, if it were not to pour out in violence and bigotry. Hobbes drew from the seventeenth-century experience of religious dissonance the straight-forward conclusion that people 'are inclined to suppose and feign unto themselves, several kinds of powers invisible, and to stand in awe of their own imaginations... making the creatures of their own fancy their gods'.[25] Hence the effect of religion on uninstructed minds was both unpredictable and dangerous, and an established church is necessary, not to secure an apostolic succession, but simply to ensure that people's religious feelings coincide, and do not give rise to the civil disorder of which Hobbes had been a horrified witness.

According to Hobbes, civil society owes its order and legitimacy to a social contract. This is a contract of each person with every other, to establish and maintain a sovereign with the authority to make laws and to enforce them against those who would otherwise defect. God has no part in this contract, since it is only when it has been struck that people have the peace and the leisure to make proper room for him. It was precisely the religion-induced defection of the subjects of King Charles I that had plunged England into civil war, and anybody truly concerned for the well-being of his fellow citizens would recognize, Hobbes believed, that the social contract must always take precedence over whatever religious enthusiasm claims some rival obedience. That, for Hobbes, was the meaning of an established church.

The Restoration saw Milton silenced and Hobbes accused of atheism by Parliament (though protected by King Charles II). The Stuart monarchy soon fell apart, with the Roman Catholic James II sent into exile. Only after the Glorious Revolution of 1688 did the

English try to unite all the fragments of their religious inheritance under the protection of a single, Protestant, and established church. Asked to swear an oath of submission to the new King William many bishops felt bound to refuse, since they had sworn the very same oath to the exiled King James. The expulsion of the non-jurors forced an alignment between Church and State that might in other circumstances have led to conflict. As it was, people were exhausted by religious quarrels, and enough bishops were prepared to revise their vows to ensure continuity of worship. Indeed, by this time the Anglican Church had become quite agile in the skill of bending principle to circumstance. And the Act of Toleration of 1689 compelled it to be more agile still, since it permitted Protestants who dissented from the Church of England – such as Baptists and Congregationalists – to worship in their own churches and according to their own conventions.

The permission was not unconditional, however, and two of the conditions – the oath of allegiance and the pledge of the supremacy of the monarch – involved the effective recognition of an established church. The other condition, rejection of the doctrine of transubstantiation, was aimed at Catholics, being not so much an outcome of the scholastic quibbles that had split the Church since Wyclif, as a symbolic affirmation of Englishness against the devious workings of the Jesuits, the Spaniards, and the Antichrist who had usurped St Peter's throne. Even Locke, who produced the neatest argument for toleration in English – the *Letter Concerning Toleration* published in the same year, 1689 – did not believe that toleration should be extended to Catholics, since their loyalty to the civil power could not be depended upon. For Locke, as for Hobbes, the achievement of Anglicanism was to have domesticated all sources of authority, the religious included, and confined them within the borders of the kingdom. The position defended explicitly by Hobbes prevailed: by defending an established church, whose precepts were moderated by a measure of toleration, the English could ensure civil peace. But what mattered first was peace; concerning doctrine and ritual a certain measure of flexibility would be possible, provided the kingdom's enemies were prevented from taking advantage of it.

This kind of compromise was often attacked in the seventeenth-century debates as Erastianism, meaning the doctrine associated (possibly wrongly) with the Swiss Protestant Erastus, according to which the State has precedence over the Church, and the right to dictate its customs. But this misrepresents what was finally achieved in 1689. Moderation and compromise, seriously jeopardized in the seventeenth-century turmoil, became the default position of English institutions. The Book of Common Prayer opens with the following well-known words:

> It hath been the wisdom of the Church of England, ever since
> the first compiling of her Publick Liturgy, to keep the mean
> between the two extremes, of too much stiffness in refusing,
> and of too much easiness in admitting any variation from it.

The call for moderation informs every page of Hooker, who is also clear that toleration is not a matter of rejecting objective truth but of accepting objective error. But just what the truth is and what the error were matters that few people by the end of the seventeenth century had the heart to discuss. The Anglican Church emerged from the smoke and gunfire as a creative muddle, a genial mixture of belief and scepticism, of Christian devotion and ironical self-doubt. It was an established church, but with a troop of Nonconformist rivals that it could neither include nor condemn. It was a Protestant institution whose members declared their faith in the 'Holy Catholick Church', using the words of the Nicene Creed. It was a part of the government of the kingdom, whose bishops sat in Parliament, and also an institution of civil society, peacefully working outside the purview of the State. It took seriously St Paul's pithy statement, that 'the powers that be are ordained of God' (Romans 13, 1), while going 'far from the madding crowd' in search of holiness. Its priesthood enjoyed a social status that attracted the younger sons of aristocratic families; but its ideal remained the Poor Parson of Chaucer, for whom all human beings are equal in the eyes of the Lord, and equal subjects of redemption. It belonged to what Bagehot was later to call the 'dignified' part of our unwritten constitution, clothing public events in ceremonial splendour, and wrapping the conduct of political life in rules and procedures that conferred an inscrutable majesty on the affairs of state. But its rules were not truly binding, and anyone could break them with impunity and still remain within the fold.

In short, the Anglican Church was not simply one community of believers among others: it had become a national way of life. It was England in its Sunday dress, entering the modern world of nationhood and Empire. It had regained the definite article, borrowed from a new kind of corporate person, one defined in terms of territory, language and law.

THREE

My Church

The town of Malmesbury sits on a hill above a bend in the River Avon, a situation that renders it easy to defend against assault, and which led the tenth-century King Athelstan, grandson of Alfred the Great, victor over the Danes and the Scots and first King of all England, to treat the town and its abbey as a favoured residence. The abbey was home to the twelfth-century monk William of Malmesbury, probably the most learned Englishman of his day, whose Chronicles of the Kings of England is an early attempt to wind together the history of our country and the localized spirit of its Church. The abbey was partly destroyed at the Dissolution, to be restored in the eighteenth century as a parish church. Stones from its ruined nave and transept appear in churches and farmhouses all around the town, including the little farmhouse, Sundey Hill Farm, where I am writing. On one side of Malmesbury lies the parish of Westport and Charlton, where the father of Thomas Hobbes was parish priest, but from which he was forced to flee, having violently assaulted (and according to some reports killed) a fellow clergyman.

We know little of Hobbes's childhood, except that he was rescued from ignorance, like so many children of the poor, by a grammar school. He left Malmesbury for Magdalen Hall, Oxford, aged fifteen, already the author of a translation of Euripides' *Medea* from Greek into Latin verse. But he remained proud of his birthplace, and always signed himself Thomas Hobbes of Malmesbury. The town, which had become prosperous from wool in the time of Henry VIII, did not recover from the destruction of its abbey and the further destruction wrought by the Civil Wars; today it is a quiet cul-de-sac, from which the memory of its former eminence has all but vanished. Hobbes was recently honoured with a small plaque marked 'Hobbes' Cottage', placed on the house of Cotswold stone on the site where he is thought to have been born. But this attempt at local patriotism was immediately negated by a facetious neighbour, who placed a similar plaque marked 'Hog's Cottage' on the house next door.

Two miles to the other side of Malmesbury lies the hamlet of Garsdon, a handful of farmhouses, a converted Victorian school, a Jacobean manor house and a sprawling rectory, all gathered around the church of All Saints. The foundations of the church tower date from the fifteenth century, though the parapet was added later, with stones taken from the half-ruined abbey. The nave was rebuilt in 1855, by the firm of Coe and Goodwin – Coe being a former apprentice of George Gilbert Scott and an efficient practitioner of Victorian Gothic. Inside the church stands the seventeenth-century memorial to Sir Lawrence Washington, squire of Garsdon Manor, and his wife. The memorial was reassembled in 1903 after many adventures, including sale to an American who had the stones boxed and labelled, but who somehow never managed to get them beyond the docks in Southampton.

The family connection with the first American president is not the only claim to fame of this tiny hamlet. Sir Lawrence Washington was an ancestor of Lady Selina Shirley, wife of the ninth Earl of Huntingdon, and leading spirit of the evangelical revival initiated by George Whitefield and John Wesley. This revival formed the most important episode in the history of Anglicanism during the eighteenth century, and it began around Malmesbury, where it was George Whitefield, John Wesley's Calvinist associate, who was the most important influence. Thanks to Whitefield, the Moravian Brethren, an evangelical sect active in the Czech lands and in Germany in the early part of the eighteenth century, were invited to establish churches in the neighbourhood. A Moravian church still operates in the nearby village of Tytherton, and another has recently closed in Malmesbury itself. Later in the eighteenth century the Wesleyan influence declined, but a re-evangelizing of the area by the Primitive Methodists in the nineteenth century led to the building of a Methodist chapel in every village. That of Garsdon – built in 1860, one of a row of Victorian cottages in stone – has now been converted into a second home. The simplest of these chapels are of corrugated iron, with wooden windows in the Gothic style, installed at a time when builders' merchants always had a store of ready-made Gothic details. One or two still hold services, with visiting preachers addressing small congregations. The members are the ageing survivors of a farming community that turned its back, during the agricultural collapse of the nineteenth century, on an official church of squires and landlords, and sought for a plain-spoken, work-endorsing faith that would dignify their poverty. Now Methodism is little more than a memory, as insignificant to the people of Malmesbury as Thomas Hobbes, their philosopher, as Joseph Addison, one of their more famous Members of Parliament, as Brother William, their historian, or as Athelstan, their once resident King.

Nonconformism was not new to Garsdon when the Methodist revival swept the countryside. Records show that two Garsdon residents – William Ridge and his son William – were presented to the Justices for failing to receive Communion on Easter Sunday, 1662, young William having denounced the new Book of Common Prayer as 'popery'. The subsequent drift away from the established church in the eighteenth and nineteenth centuries was, however, more the result of pastoral neglect than popular dissent. Garsdon Church and its tithes were often acquired by a non-resident rector. One such, Joseph Simpson, received the living in absentia from 1763 until 1797. Another non-resident, T. A. Methuen, was rector from 1814 until 1869. (At that time the Lords Methuen were in possession of Garsdon Manor, had the 'gift' of the living, and could, therefore, bestow it on whichever useless relative was most in need of a sinecure.) Understandably, one of Joseph Simpson's curates, John Davis, who was paid a pittance to perform the duties that the Rev. Simpson was too grand and too far away to bother with, turned Congregationalist, being active in founding a Congregational church in Malmesbury in 1780, when the town was represented in

Parliament by another famous man, Charles James Fox, who did not care a damn about churches, whatever their creed. (It should be said that, as residents of a 'rotten borough', the people of Malmesbury had little say in electing their representative.)

The transformation of the Anglican Church from a pastoral to a pecuniary institution – so that it seemed, for a while, like a kind of welfare system for the upper classes – has left a lasting stain on its reputation, not least because Trollope's Barchester novels went so cleanly and beautifully to the root of the problem. But already when Trollope was writing, the Pluralities Act of 1838 had forbidden the worst of the abuses, preventing clergymen from accumulating livings as the board-member classes today accumulate directorships. And it was a rural parson, Charles Kingsley, who at the time was busy reminding the Church of its mission towards the downtrodden and the oppressed.

Although neither downtrodden nor oppressed, Garsdon's vicar today is certainly no richer than the poorest of his congregation. His church is one of those tranquil places described by Philip Larkin – a serious place on serious earth, standing on a grassy knoll among lichen-covered tombstones. It is one of six churches under the direction of a single rector, who also has charge of Lea, Brinkworth, Dauntsey and Great and Little Somerford. Garsdon offers a regular Sunday service to a congregation of fifteen that swells to fifty at Easter and Christmas. Holy Communion is celebrated once a month, and every now and then a wedding, a funeral or a baptism returns this place to its former position, as the centre of a Christian community. For the last fifteen years I have attended this church as organist, playing the instrument installed in 1903, which has one manual, three stops and no pedals.

Garsdon Church is not exactly typical of Anglicanism today: it has opted to use the Book of Common Prayer in its services, and some members of its congregation, when asked to read the lesson, will bring a copy of the King James Bible to the lectern, to place it on top of the New English Bible that is kept there. The appearance of the New English Bible some forty years ago was received by many Anglicans in something like the way Tyndale's Bible was received by the Holy See. But things have changed since then, and the church I describe in this chapter has put on a set of informal outer garments that to some extent conceal its starched inner soul.

Churchgoing people are of two kinds. There are those who feel the presence of God in their lives, who devote time to prayer and meditation and who make an offering of their work. Such people are invoked in a favourite Victorian hymn, setting words by George Herbert:

> All may of thee partake:
> Nothing can be so mean
> Which with this tincture: for thy sake
> Will not grow bright and clean.

> A servant with this clause
> Makes drudgery divine:
> Who sweeps a room as for Thy laws
> Makes that and the action fine.

The Anglican Church has a place in our literature not only as the safe career of younger sons and the easy way to social advancement. It features in such incomparable devotional poems as the Holy Sonnets of John Donne, the hymns of Herbert and Vaughan, and T. S. Eliot's 'Little Gidding'. It features in the portrait of the Christian community and its trials, such as that painted by the Rev. George Crabbe, and in the passionate calls for spiritual renewal of Ruskin and the Rossettis. It would not have endured or triumphed over its Puritan and Nonconformist rivals had it been without the reservoir of holiness that lies at its heart, or had it been deprived of the energy of its more passionate adherents. But it also confines that energy within socially acceptable bounds, and what is socially acceptable changes from decade to decade and from year to year. As a national church, entrusted with an ever more secular community, it has been aware for three centuries that most churchgoers are not of the spiritual kind: they are people who only fleetingly feel the presence of God in their lives, and who wish to be on the right side of him with the minimum of effort, the people described by Trollope and catered for by the intrigues and deals of Barchester.

For such people prayer in church is like courtesy in business: a way of maintaining a frictionless flow of spiritual goods and services. They would not put up for long with a priesthood that unceasingly reminded them of their worthlessness, and it has been the wisdom of the Anglican establishment to ensure that such people obtain, on the whole, the kind of ministry that retains them within the fold of the Church. Trollope's unforgettable portrait of Dr Proudie, the time-serving, hen-pecked Bishop of Barchester,

reminds us too that those clergymen who fall short of the full spiritual involvement of a Wyclif, a Herbert or a Donne have found,
within the Church of England, sufficient reward to apply their very
necessary talents and ambitions to keeping the show on the road.

For it is difficult for a church to minister to the spiritually
second-rate. The temptation is to demand of everyone the enthusiasm that the many can simulate, but only the few possess. The
genius of the Roman Catholic Church has been in catering for
the majority, drawing the ordinary malefactor into the shared need
for sacramental moments, and requiring penance, atonement and
forgiveness of everyone, without disdain towards those who find it
hard to say sorry or who are quick to take revenge. This feature,
which to the ardent Puritan is a profound spiritual fault and a sign
of corruption, is – from another and more lenient perspective – a
social and political virtue. No church can hope to be a national
church if it does not emulate this aspect of the Catholic tradition.
And that is what the Anglican Church has done. It is why it prompts
continuous rebellion from the Nonconformist and the Puritan, and
also why it has had the support of ordinary people aware of their
weaknesses.

Calvin had another way of dealing with spiritual indolence,
which was to suppose that the division between the saved and the
damned had been established already by God. The fervent believer
gives proof thereby that he is a member of the elect, and a kind of
spiritual competition arises, among members of the Calvinist community, to establish a claim to a title already conferred by God, but
not yet revealed to those who worship him. The Calvinist doctrine

of predestination serves, in some such way, to keep a whole religious community on its spiritual toes, offering hope to all, but also justifying a cruel casting off of the proven sinners. Readers of James Hogg's *Confessions of a Justified Sinner* (1824) will recognize the contours of a spiritual athleticism that ruled for two or more centuries in Geneva and Scotland, but which was defeated by the Anglican Church in the days of Elizabeth I. Suffice it to say that the devotional impulse was domesticated by our Church, confined to Nonconformist movements that could be comprehended within the broad settlement of 1689.

John Wesley (1703–91), unlike his associate George Whitefield, was not a Calvinist. Indeed he emphasized the Arminian legacy of the English Church and taught 'grace abounding' to all sinners, in the spirit of Bunyan. Hence he was able to preach from within the Anglican Communion, and to recruit his following without requiring them to renounce their Anglican obedience. He took care to call his meetings at times that would not clash with Anglican services, and when the Methodist 'connections' finally coalesced as a church, it was because Wesley, deeply concerned that the Church of England had not been able to consecrate the priests then desperately needed in America, had sent priests of his own creation – describing them, however, not as priests but as ministers. (It was only in 1818, twenty years after its founder's death, that the Wesleyan Church adopted the title 'Reverend' to endorse its preachers, and by that time the Methodist movement had split.)

The history of Methodism deeply influenced the way in which Anglicanism evolved in modern times, and I will briefly return to it.

In the parish of Garsdon, however, as in so many rural parishes round about, the Anglican Church emerged from the Wesleyan crisis in the same way that the Roman Catholic Church emerged from the Reformation in France: as the reliable companion of the ordinary sinner, a ritualized portrait of a God who demands more from us than we can easily give, but not more from us than we *can* give.

In our little church at Garsdon that aspect of Anglican worship is taken for granted. This does not mean that our devotions are mere hypocrisy. It is part of the baneful legacy of Puritanism that it demands absolute proof of sincerity at every moment, sees formal gestures as a denial of personal commitment, and fails to recognize the truth in Oscar Wilde's remark, that in matters of the greatest importance it is style and not sincerity that counts. Our church is a home, a place of refuge from the undisciplined world. It is embellished with flowers, embroidered kneelers and polished brass oddments; it has the comforting smell of damp plaster, snuffed candles and Brasso. The few plaques in the walls bear local names, and celebrate virtues earned by dying. Behind the altar, set in the wall of plain dressed limestone, is a tiled reredos, on which the words 'This do, in remembrance of Me' are displayed in gilded Gothic letters. (Why 'This do', I wonder, when the Bible and the Prayer Book have 'Do this'?) The panel is edged with a vaguely art nouveau pattern of vines and grape-clusters, like the shop sign of some Edwardian wine merchant. But the reredos is a reminder that this is a Catholic church, which dispenses salvation as a daily sacrament, and which turns our thoughts to remembrance. Those six words on the wall contain the secret of tradition. What matters, they tell us, is the past, its daily re-enactment, and the intertwining threads of memory that make that past forever present among us. Our lives are wrapped around the solid fact of Christ's sacrifice like ivy around a stone. And when we gather on a Sunday it is not in order to judge the quality of devotion in our sinful neighbours, but to accept, for a while, the shortcomings that impair our weekday relations and to share the vision of an 'eternal home'.

The 1662 Book of Common Prayer provides the words of the liturgy; it provides words for the sacraments – for Baptism and Holy Communion – along with words for the rites of passage – confirmation, marriage and the burial of the dead – in which the demand for holiness is most keenly felt. It contains a Psalter, using Myles Coverdale's sixteenth-century translation of the Psalms. Coverdale was not very proficient in Hebrew or Greek and based his translation on existing modern versions (including those of Tyndale and Luther) as well as on the Latin Vulgate. But it is Coverdale's Psalms that had been sung in the Elizabethan Church, and which were most often set to music in the seventeenth century, by Lawes, Purcell and Orlando Gibbons. Hence the editors of the 1662 Prayer Book retained them, aware of the damage already done to the choirs by the abolition of Latin. And although Coverdale's happiest turns of phrase (often deriving from Tyndale) were incorporated into the King James Bible, his Psalms have a peculiar limpid quality of their own. Even when spoken – as by our cracked old voices in the pews of Garsdon – they are like spontaneous utterances before the throne of God.

Our Prayer Book and Bible did for English what the Torah did for Hebrew, what the Church fathers did for Greek and Latin and what Muhammad's recitals did for Arabic. They made our language into one fit to be spoken by God, and gave us words that could be used in the presence of the Almighty. More: they gave us words that could be used to each other, when solemnity and sacrifice require us to look each other not in the eyes only, but in the soul – as when the bridegroom promises 'to love and to cherish, till death us do part, according to God's holy ordinance'. They help us to confess our faults, to ask for forgiveness, to seek God's blessing and to know that, when we do these things, we are in touch with what is deepest in us. When the churchgoers of Garsdon confess that they 'have erred and strayed from thy ways like lost sheep' and that they have 'followed too much the devices and desires of [their] own hearts', they do not merely put themselves in touch, through the homely imagery, with those early forms of husbandry that overcame the soul-destroying regime of the hunter-gatherer. They also give exact words to the deviousness of sin – reminding themselves that sin comes from desire, that it works through 'devices', and that the source of these devices is the heart. It is an inspiring exercise to go through the words of Morning Prayer and to measure your life against them. At every point they say something both simple and true, which goes to the root of moral sentiment.

Perhaps it needed the experience of religious conflict to inspire the words of the Second Collect. For there is surely no more delicate, succinct or suggestive expression in English of the longing for peace:

O God, who art the author of peace and lover of concord, in knowledge of whom standeth our eternal life, whose service is perfect freedom; Defend us thy humble servants in all assaults of our enemies; that we, surely trusting in thy defence, may not fear the power of any adversaries, through the might of Jesus Christ our Lord.

The phrase 'whose service is perfect freedom' is a rebuke directed to those who think that freedom and authority are in conflict, and who therefore feel entitled to disturb the civil order for the sake of their spiritual liberation. And the whole implies that faith in the 'author of peace and lover of concord' is never an act of aggression but at most a defence against it.

The Prayer Book service for the burial of the dead, including fragments from the Bible, knitted together with a kind of liturgical panache that may well be unique to the Anglican tradition, contains many sublime passages, such as this:

Man that is born of a woman hath but a short time to live, and is full of misery. He cometh up, and is cut down, like a flower; he fleeth as it were a shadow, and never continueth in one stay. In the midst of life we are in death: of whom may we seek succour, but of thee, O Lord, who for our sins art justly displeased?

Those words have come down to us in part from the Old Testament, in part from a hymn composed by an eleventh-century German monk; but the alchemy of the Prayer Book has turned their leaden sentiments into a nugget of gold, a gift offered to all of us at the graveside, uniting us with the one who is being buried, and consecrating his loss.

In such passages you encounter the real achievement of the Prayer Book, which is the achievement of sacramental religion everywhere – namely, the consecration of ordinary life, and the opening of the heart to seriousness. For there are two aspects of religion that should be clearly distinguished if we are to understand the Christian faith. Christianity offers another life; but it also sanctifies the present one. Platonic philosophy shaped the Christian hope, Judaism the Christian blessing. The whole purpose of the Jewish law is to consecrate daily life. Such is the deeper meaning of the Sabbath – the call to stand back from getting and spending, to enter the condition of contemplation in which subject and object coalesce, to be useful beyond utility, and so to see through the veil of appetite to the sacred core of our being. The Roman Catholic Church inherited the Jewish concept of the sacred, and thanks largely to Cranmer the sacramental essence of the Catholic faith was passed into English, given liturgical authority, and captured for the new community of believers – the community whose spiritual unity in the Church would be the consecration of their unity as a nation. Hence our Church remained *the* Church, the Church of the Apostolic Succession, whose offices could claim the spiritual continuity on which the sacraments depend.

Between them, therefore, Tyndale and Cranmer created that extraordinary idiom that enabled the English to endow the objects

and institutions of their world with a nimbus of home-grown sanctity. Some of this idiom has passed into everyday speech: 'the fat of
the land', 'men of renown', 'in the land of Nod', 'a fool's Paradise',
'scapegoat' and so on, from Tyndale; 'miserable sinners', 'the world,
the flesh and the devil', 'the time of our tribulation' and similar,
from Cranmer. But much of Biblical and liturgical English remains
apart from the common tongue – influencing it and influenced by
it, but discreetly haloed, nevertheless, as it works its miracles in the
everyday world. Words like 'almighty' and 'everlasting', phrases
like 'the author of peace and the lover of concord', transfigure the
things and situations to which they are applied. They are familiar,
dignified words, which lose nothing from repetition. Armed with
their sound and syntax, our congregation in Garsdon is never at a
loss for prayer. And liturgical English endows us with a mysterious
key to God's presence – the archaic 'thou' that makes the most
binding intimacy into another and holier form of remoteness.

And here it is worth reminding ourselves of the very great
difficulty of prayer. A prayer, composed from the words of this
world, must nevertheless aim beyond this world. Rooted in the most
intense personal feeling it must nevertheless achieve the kind of
impersonal objectivity that permits anyone to say it with conviction.
Prayers are the most universal of all literary forms, since they enter
common usage only if all people can utter them, knowing what they
mean, and knowing that their own lives are touched and comprehended by them. Prayers both consecrate and simplify the occasions
of their use, as when Christians precede a meal with the words 'For
what we are about to receive, may the Lord make us truly thankful',

or when Muslim Arabs begin a speech with the words '*bism illah il-raHmân il-raHîm*', the two aspirated 'ha's forming an outrush of spirit that every speaker of the language can feel. A poem survives in the anthologies because it is loved by some; a prayer survives in daily life because it is needed by everyone. Great religious leaders establish their place in people's hearts by giving them words of comfort, as did Christ, Muhammad and the Buddha. And to alter those words is to threaten the foundation of faith. Hence the medieval maxim, '*lex orandi, lex credendi*' – the law of prayer is the law of belief.

A well-known Victorian hymn by J. Montgomery expresses the point:

> Lord, teach us how to pray aright
> With reverence and with fear;
> Though dust and ashes in thy sight,
> We may, we must, draw near.

The Prayer Book is there to answer this appeal, and it beautifully succeeds. Its prayers are objective, universal, supposing no metaphysical sophistication or dramatic subtlety in those who utter them but summoning only the heartfelt trust in God. Spiritually burdened sages often compose interesting prayers, but rarely can these prayers be uttered by ordinary people who seek to put themselves right with their Maker. Here is part of a prayer by Kierkegaard:

Father in Heaven! To You the congregation often makes its petition for all who are sick and sorrowful, and when someone among us lies ill, alas, of mortal sickness, the congregation sometimes desires a special petition; grant that we may each one of us become in good time aware what sickness it is which is the sickness unto death and aware that we are all of us suffering from this sickness.

Probably only someone who has read Kierkegaard's *The Sickness Unto Death* (1849) will fully understand what the prayer is getting at. Kierkegaard's prayers are soaked in metaphysical anguish, and it is no small achievement on the part of Samuel Barber (a Presbyterian believer) to have set some of them to music in one of the great cantatas of recent times. Kierkegaard's prayers may be set to lasting music, but they will never be kept in the ordinary heart.

It is the language of the Book of Common Prayer and the King James Bible that the English Church has held in trust, and which forms, in my view, the real essence of its religion. Historians continue to argue over the causes of the seventeenth-century turmoil to which I alluded in the last chapter. But the literature of the time makes abundantly clear that the sound and syntax of the Bible gave shape to the prevailing bellicosity. It was an age when truth seemed more important than compromise, and when the settlement envisaged in the Thirty-nine Articles was suddenly under threat. Englishmen could now shout at one another in God's tone of voice, and this lent exultation to their anger. But the very fact that the language was a common possession led at last to a renewed attempt at compromise. And in the event it was compromise that won. The imposition of the Act of Uniformity in 1662 led to the departure of some nine hundred ministers from the Church of England. But within six decades the Nonconforming congregations had won the right to build their own churches, and the language heard in them was the old liturgical idiom of Tyndale and Cranmer.

Hence we find the evangelical John Wesley addressing his followers in the same idiolect as the popish Edward Pusey. Both were Anglicans; each defended a faith that he called 'catholic'. Wesley, advocating scriptural worship and union with a God-fearing congregation, describes the true catholic as:

> one who, retaining these blessings with the strictest care, keeping them as the apple of his eye, at the same time loves, – as friends, as brethren in the Lord, as members of Christ and children of God, as joint-partakers now of the present kingdom of God, and fellow-heirs of his eternal kingdom – all, of whatever opinion, or worship, or congregation, who believe in the Lord Jesus Christ.[26]

And this magnanimous gesture of toleration is so shaped by the English Bible as scarcely to be told apart from it. The words ('brethren', 'partakers', 'kingdom') are Biblical; the idioms and allusions too are Biblical or liturgical ('apple of his eye', for example, is from Deuteronomy 32, 10; 'members of Christ' is from the catechism in the Book of Common Prayer, and ultimately from St Paul), and the whole is presented in the same spirit of compromise as is declared in the opening sentence of the Prayer Book.

The beauties of the King James Bible and Cranmer's Prayer Book need no new commentary from me. But often, reflecting behind the curtain that hides the organist from the congregation of Garsdon Church, I find myself wrestling with the concept of the sacred, and asking myself how it is that words can consecrate. It is as though, through their beauty and solemnity, the words of our traditional services bow down to touch the things they refer to. In the Hindu tradition life is consecrated by immersion – whether in the waters of the Ganges or in *puja*, the rituals that form the framework of daily life. The Roman Catholic Church inherited from antiquity a similar habit of consecrating life through pious observances: the lighting of lamps, the laying out of offerings, the genuflecting, crossing, bowing and whispering that change the place where they occur from an empirical to a transcendental location. But the Protestant spirit rebels against those habits. And it rebels on behalf of the word.

The word is the instrument of thought. For the Protestant spirit, gestures and rituals conceal reality, words reveal it. Words are the enemy of superstition and the torch that lights our spiritual path. For the extreme Protestant, therefore, words are enough, and a dialogue of friends in the Meeting House is all the holiness that a Quaker requires. The Anglican Church is more cautious, and also more subtle. It recognizes that, when it comes to worship, words must *conjure* their subject and not just describe it. They must be lifted out of their everyday and conversational use, to become ritual gestures, invocations rather than descriptions. Words used at the altar are like spells: they are being used not to describe the world but to change it. Thus in the Eucharist words do not describe a primeval sacrifice. They make it present.[27]

The Gospel of St John tells us in its opening verse that 'in the beginning was the Word, and the Word was with God, and the Word was God'. Verse 14 adds that 'the Word was made flesh, and dwelt among us, (and we beheld his glory, the glory as of the only begotten of the Father,) full of grace and truth.' Those verses owe their deep meaning to a single word, *logos*, which our Bible translates as 'word', and the Vulgate as '*verbum*'. But *logos* is a term with a history: in Greek philosophy it means reason, explanation or account – hence 'logic'. St John is telling us that the world has an explanation, that the explanation is God, and that God has revealed himself in human form. He is using the idea of Reason to express the mystery of Faith, and in doing so conveys what is meant by the 'Word of God' – namely, God communing with himself. We cannot directly understand what this might be: it is one part of the 'peace of God, which passeth all understanding', as the Prayer Book puts it, quoting from St Paul in the King James Version (Philippians 4, 7). But St John's way of expressing the central tenet of the Christian faith opens the way both to the Catholic emphasis on the Eucharistic mystery and to the Protestant emphasis on the Word.

The Anglican belief is that there is a tension, but not a conflict, between those two. The Church of England is a Protestant church, which accepts that holy things should be described and explained in intelligible language. The influence of Calvin and his Commentaries permeates the thinking of the early Anglican divines. But their church is also a Catholic church, which accepts the authority of traditional usage, and which believes that words must be care-fully prepared if they are to put us in touch with the Almighty. Words can take us into the presence of God only when they are lifted out of their normal usage, and given solemn movement and dignified dress. Hence the liturgy of our Church was no sooner chosen than it solidified, adopting the aspect of eternity.

This solidification of language is a feature of durable liturgies and prayers in every religion. The Roman Catholic Mass is still introduced with Greek words that survive from the first liturgies of the Hellenistic Christians: *Kyrie eleison, Christe eleison*. Latin remained the vehicle of the Mass, long after it had ceased to be the vernacular used outside the Church. The rituals of the Mass purport to be eternal, ways of acknowledging what does not exist in time and which, therefore, cannot be explained but only re-enacted. Words used at the altar do not clarify what is done, they *do* it. To demand that these words be uttered in a language intelligible to everyone is to threaten the only authority that rituals can conceiv-ably possess, which is the authority of long-established usage. Rituals are understood only by those who see that they need no explanation and that they must not be changed.

The happy compromise hit upon by Cranmer was to provide vernacular words that, for all their simplicity and clarity, sound to the ordinary English ear as though they have not been invented but revealed. The combination of Calvin-influenced clarity, Psalm-like imagery and the rhythms of courtly English show the English language speaking from another world and in another voice. To the Elizabethan worshipper Cranmer's words were new: but they were accepted as the sound of forever, and not the sound of now. Their audible essence is one of repetition, and their effect is that of the Hindu *mantra*, lifting their speakers out of the here and now and bringing them face to face with that which never changes. It is this feature of the Prayer Book and the King James Bible that is responsible for the durability of our Church. Hence the replacement of those texts with versions that make no attempt to emulate their high-toned solemnity but which have all the specious ease of a TV chat show is, whether cause or effect, a mark of that Church's decline.

The 1662 Prayer Book was imposed by an Act of Uniformity, and the King James Bible was until recently 'appointed to be read in churches'. Not surprisingly, therefore, those texts have profoundly influenced the speeches, poems and invocations that have been composed for official occasions over the last three centuries. From Wilberforce through Gladstone to Enoch Powell, the House of Commons has enjoyed a continuous sequence of 'Prayer Book Politicians', who have used Cranmer's turns of phrase to round the corners of their speeches and add a measure of timeless validity even to the most immediate and ephemeral of decisions. The influence of the Psalms on Churchill's wartime speeches is well known, as is the influence of Cranmer on Lawrence Binyon, whose poem 'For the Fallen', written at the height of the First World War, now occupies a more or less official place in the Anglican liturgy, having supplied a need that could not be met by the Prayer Book – the need to face up to a slaughter so vast and so senseless, that not even the Civil Wars had provided us with an intelligible precedent. Binyon's words are repeated at every Service of Remembrance all across the former British Empire, and are affixed to war memorials in churches and village squares around our country:

> They shall grow not old, as we that are left grow old:
> Age shall not weary them, nor the years condemn.
> At the going down of the sun and in the morning,
> We will remember them.

Those words are spoken every Remembrance Sunday in Garsdon Church, as we stand to face the plaque on which the names of the fallen are written – names of farming families round about. They are words with the same simple and incontrovertible nature as the words chosen by Cranmer: words that do not merely bear repetition but that are made to be repeated, like the song of some territorial bird. Such is the essential character of liturgical language. And the same is true of so much that is memorable in our recent literature. The most solemn passages in D. H. Lawrence, Thomas Hardy, T. S. Eliot and the lesser figures that emulated them are, as it were, suspended on the frame made by the King James Bible and the Book of Common Prayer.

Although Garsdon has retained the 1662 Prayer Book it is not a high or 'Anglo-Catholic' church. It simply preserves the memory of an established habit of solemnization, which English people of my generation encountered in church and chapel, in school and college, in Scouts and Guides, indeed in every place or gathering where the voice of authority arose – as it arose then naturally – among ordinary people inoffensively perpetuating their national sentiment.

Thus my first encounters with the religion of the English were at school. In both primary school and secondary school the day would begin with an assembly, in which lessons were read, prayers offered and hymns sung, to the accompaniment of a piano played by a member of staff. The words used were invariably those of the King James Bible and the Book of Common Prayer, and when we said the Lord's Prayer it was to Our Father *which* art in heaven, with a promise to forgive *them that* trespass against us.[28] Those peculiar idioms seemed to have no other explanation than the unfathomable holiness of the being to whom they were addressed, and this effect was only enhanced by the fact that God spoke and was spoken to in a language that was both richer, more ceremonial and in a strange way more intimate than any used among ourselves.

My parents were sensible people who had lived through the war and come to the conclusion that no God could possibly have permitted it. As far as my mother was concerned, that was the end of the matter. But it was not the end of the matter for my father, who had been brought up among Nonconformists, saved from starvation by the Salvation Army, and constantly offended by the Anglican Church, which his mother had forced him to attend, and which for him was one arm of the ruling conspiracy that cast a shadow over England. Like many of his generation, my father looked inwards to find the seams of the Cromwellian Rebellion still exposed on the surface of his soul. Religion, for him, was a matter of taking sides in the great class war that defined our national history. In this he was true to the Anglican settlement – true, not because he dissented from the theological doctrines of our Church, but because he

acknowledged the Anglican Church as an attempt to claim dominion over the English – acknowledged it and rejected it. He wished
his children to graduate to atheism from a heritage of Nonconformist resentment. That way they would acquire a healthy
contempt for robes and chasubles and rood screens, for toffee-nosed
vicars and the gentry in their private pews. My sisters and I were
sent first to a Methodist chapel, where we encountered the hymns,
lessons and prayers that were already familiar from school, and
then, when this experience seemed not to improve us, to a Baptist
chapel, a place so cold and bleak and forlorn that my parents never
set foot there.

The Baptist chapel offered services of a confused and mysterious kind. We knew that they were preparations for the terrible
ordeal in which, it was rumoured, we would be forced to plunge
naked into a tank of water, before a crowd of onlookers so purified
by their own immersion as to be able to stare at a naked body
without sin (a feat of which we, by contrast, would be forever incapable). The thought of this ordeal gave a peculiar urgency to the
Biblical instruction, conducted by a slow-spoken old man who was
a carpenter by trade, and whose horny fingers with their blackened
creases and broken nails conveyed, as they traced the verses on
those India-paper pages, such a weight of simple trust and piety that
I was touched in spite of myself, and would often put all my pocket
money into the velvet collection pouch that came round at the
end of the class. And this Bible whose verses we explored one by
one, as they emerged from beneath the fingers of Piers Plowman,
was the very Bible whose solemn turns of phrase would frame our

speech days at school. At the first sign that the regime of parental vigilance was slackening, however, we escaped from the Baptist yoke and joined the company of unbelievers. My father did not insist, assuming that we had acquired the rudiments of proletarian religion and would now be safe from the encroachment of a forbidden holiness.

But the forbidden holiness stalked us, like God himself. You had only to turn to see its face, following your movements with strange, occupied eyes that were immediately averted when it saw itself seen. I rejected the Baptist Church because it was nothing, for me, save doctrine. Yet all around was something else – not a doctrine or a morality but a call to membership. High Wycombe, where I grew up, was surrounded then by sleepy hamlets and half-vacant villages, each with its Norman or Early English church of flint and stone. And in these churches a peculiar silence had been stored, along with the embroidered kneelers and the Victorian altar cloths with their gold and emerald fabrics, like robes left behind by some visiting angel. You could not ignore these places. My father too was drawn to them, for he was a country-lover, a disciple of H. J. Massingham, who believed that the material progress that had benefitted the capitalist class had also robbed the people of their country, and if unopposed would rob the country of its soul. He sought out that soul in rural lanes and shady churchyards, where you could contemplate the beauty of a landscape made in the image of the Anglican God, who in turn (for an atheist like my father) had been made in the image of the landscape. And when we moved from High Wycombe, then fast becoming a suburb of London, to Marlow, on the Thames, I found myself living next door to a church that had tried to catch hold of that God as he flitted all but unobserved between the villages.

I began, aged fifteen, to attend All Saints' Church in Marlow. My father believed that I went each Sunday morning to the Baptist chapel, having inexplicably rediscovered a desire to inspect my sins. I excused the lie, since it was told on God's behalf. But it was also a fitting apprenticeship in the English religion that I should begin my devotions from a posture of pretence. Marlow Church is itself a pretence: a large, Gothic Revival structure in flint and stone, designed to look as though it had stood forever at the end of a High Street where it was, in fact, the newest building.

Until Nikolaus Pevsner came on the scene, and intimidated the English with censorious German scholarship, the Gothic Revival had been accepted as an integral part of the English settlement, a good-natured attempt to ensure that God found suitable accommodation in the country that was his. Of course, the revival made an impact on the continent – but it was with isolated and showy monuments such as the Hungarian Parliament. Only in England and its colonies did Neo-Gothic architecture fulfil its spiritual mission, as an unassuming vernacular idiom that re-made the landscape as something ancient and immune to change. It was a deeply moral architecture, composed in a syntax that deliberately denied the 'satanic mills' that made it possible, just as Biblical English denied the everyday speech of those who used it in their worship. And, having established its legitimacy in ecclesiastical use, the Neo-Gothic style rapidly spread through the culture, encrusting factories, law courts, schools, colleges, water works, railway stations and houses with fairytale pinnacles and dreaming towers. To the visiting architectural historian it had turned the English towns and cities into vast arenas of pretence, as hypocritical in their appearance as in the religious manners that the buildings signified. To the English, however, the Gothic Revival was simply a new way to reaffirm their ownership of England, and to restore their country to its true condition of enchantment.

And this charge of hypocrisy – so often made by foreigners, and endorsed from time to time by the English themselves – should be viewed from the Anglican perspective. A hypocrite is someone who pretends to believe something, or to feel something, in order to score some advantage by deception. English religion was not, in that sense, hypocritical, any more than good manners are hypocritical, even though they involve conventional expressions of goodwill that could not possibly stand up to interrogation. The intention has not been to deceive, still less to score an advantage, but to collaborate in the work of re-enchantment – the work that began in 1689, when a century of violent conflict had persuaded the English people that, when kindness is opposed by conviction, it is conviction that must go.

For this reason 'we have in England,' as Garsdon's former Member of Parliament, Joseph Addison, put it in 1712, 'a particular bashfulness in everything that regards religion'.[29] The topic of religion, which had become embarrassing by the end of the seventeenth century, was even more so to Englishmen of my generation, as unmentionable as sex or love or hygiene. Like patriotism, of which it was a part, the English religion has been, during the three centuries of establishment, placed beyond question. This is not because people did not question it – on the contrary. It is because it is common knowledge that there is nothing to be gained from doing so. The English know in their hearts that faith is in large part a human invention – the whole history of their Church reminds them of this. By the end of the eighteenth century they had settled, according to Hume, 'into the most cool indifference with regard to religious matters that is to be found in any nation in the world'. Hume may have been exaggerating; but the census of 1851 showed that by then only 50 per cent of the English were regular worshippers – a figure that dropped to 25 per cent in some city areas. It is with only slight exaggeration that Orwell could write in 1941 that:

the common people [of England] are without definite religious belief, and have been so for centuries. The Anglican Church never had a real hold on them, it was simply a preserve of the landed gentry, and the Nonconformist sects only influenced minorities. And yet they have retained a deep tinge of Christian feeling, while almost forgetting the name of Christ.[30]

But this 'tinge of Christian feeling' had a source, and that source was the Anglican Church, whose messages were not shouted in English ears like the harangues of the Ranters and the Puritans, but filtered through the landscape, through the web of spires, pinnacles and finials that stitched the townscape to the sky, through the hymns, carols and oratorios that rang out in all their assemblies, and through that fragment of the Prayer Book that they recited each day, promising to 'forgive those who trespass against us', and never sure quite what the word 'trespass' really means. Hence it was no hypocrisy that led them automatically to put 'C. of E.' on any form enquiring after their religion, or to acknowledge the necessity of religion in every ceremony in which their loyalties were rehearsed. Their religion has been a conscious artefact. Like good manners, it does not bear too close an interrogation. It has been a collective polishing of the world, and has veneered the ordinary life of England in the way that a smile veneers a face. Of course, it had not started that way, as my brief history in the last chapter was designed to show. But that is the way it was in our greatest and most peaceful periods.

Marlow Church had a 'high church' vicar, with a double-barrelled name (Vaughan-Wilkes) and an upper-class voice, who lived in the old rectory beside the churchyard. His services were conducted to the letter of the Book of Common Prayer, and his sermons were elaborations of its poetry. His wife was the daughter of the Very Rev. Cyril Argentine Alington, Anglican divine, headmaster of Eton, and author of many famous hymns, including 'Good Christian men, rejoice and sing!'. The Rev. Vaughan-Wilkes had himself been a master at Eton, and then headmaster at Radley, before entering the Church. He was a holy and humble man, who had for many years practised his vocation among miners, refusing ecclesiastical preferment, and spending his energies in charitable work. For me, however, he was a symbol of the Anglican establishment and a representative of its peculiar charm.

Marlow was a church that prided itself on doing things properly. Robed choirboys sang in procession, leading the Rev. Vaughan-Wilkes to the altar in his flowing chasuble like cherubs drawing some airborne god. The mystery of the Catholic faith wafted around the altar, while the old Protestant call to duty resounded through the hymns. The Psalms were chanted by the choir in that peculiar tuneless and metreless idiom, by means of which the Anglican Church retained the mesmerism of plainsong while carefully removing all traces of its ascetic meaning. The organist began and ended with voluntaries, drawing extensively on the French repertoire (Franck, Widor and Vierne), which released an ineffable loneliness – the loneliness of the organ loft itself, a simulacrum of which I was later to experience in Garsdon – into the space of the church, muffling every soul that knelt there. And during Communion the organist would improvise on muted pipes whimsical watery sequences, full of fifths and fourths in the manner of Vaughan Williams and Herbert Howells. It was as though the Holy Ghost himself were present, humming quietly to himself in an English accent.

The atmosphere of those old Anglican services, which I despair of capturing in words, since it was so much a matter of things unexplained and now inexplicable, haunted me through ensuing years. For a while I saw Christianity in general and Anglicanism in particular as a retreat from reality, a way of hiding from the modern world and taking comfort in a Saviour whose unbelievable promises had long ago been discredited. I was, for most of my adult life, seldom more than a half believer, and the half of me that believed was drawn more to the Roman than the English Church. Gradually, however, I came to understand that my feeling for England could not draw back from the Church that has been the repository of its spirit, that the atmosphere that has haunted me is full of a meaning that it is my duty to explore, and that its message has been kept alive by people far wiser and better than I am. The decision to respond to Garsdon's need for an organist was, for me, a natural part of a larger decision, which was to settle down in my native country, and to be as much a part of things as my nature allows – which is, I am sorry to say, not very much.

Garsdon has lost many of the features that endured in Marlow: there is no longer Evensong, that most beautiful of all the Anglican services, but now disappearing almost everywhere. There is no choir, and we speak the Psalms antiphonally with only the dimmest recognition of what 'antiphonal' means. Although we have kept the Book of Common Prayer, bidding prayers jaggedly inserted into the prayer 'for the whole state of Christ's church militant here in earth' destroy what to me is the clearest and most moving of all the Anglican invocations. And yet and yet… Looking back over the half century since I last attended the church at Marlow, I know, when I sit behind the organist's curtain in Garsdon, that not only am I the same person as the timid boy who first understood that his country is not just an ordinary place in time but one with a replica in eternity, but also that this is the same Church in which I knelt to take my first Communion.

Two of the things that unite Marlow and Garsdon eloquently express the syncretism of the Anglican Church: architecture and music. The leading talent of the Gothic Revival, Augustus Pugin, was only just an Englishman, and also a fervent convert to the Roman Catholic faith. But his message, relayed in stentorian tones by John Ruskin, quickly became part of the English idea. The Gothic was the style that would help the English religion to reconquer the landscape, to overreach the mean and unsacramental chapels of the Nonconformists, and to regain the faithless cities for their Church.

The growth of the manufacturing towns had created an opportunity for the Methodists, Baptists and Independents that they did not neglect. The diocesan nature of the Anglican Church meant that ordination to the priesthood, and the consecration of churches, were slow and intricate processes, with many appointments requiring the approval of the monarch on Parliamentary advice, and many livings remaining in the gift of distant grandees. Thus the living of Westport, once enjoyed and abused by the father of Thomas Hobbes, was in the gift of the Lord Chancellor. (Visiting Malmesbury in 1867, the writer Richard Jefferies noted that the living was worth £320 plus residence – enough to maintain a clergyman and his family in considerable style.) During the whole of the eighteenth century only ten new churches were built in London. By 1800, as a result of unprecedented demographic changes, Marylebone parish had swollen to 60,000 residents, while its sole Anglican church had only 900 seats. At the end of the Napoleonic wars there were 2,423 parishes in England and Wales without an incumbent. The Nonconformists, whose congregations could build places of worship and appoint preachers on their own initiative, experienced no such deprivation. Over a thousand meeting houses were built in the reign of William III alone. In 1715 there were thirty-five Independent churches in Wales; by 1868 there were 766 and by 1920 well over a thousand, by which time 'chapel' had replaced 'church' as the place of Welsh religion.

Parliament eventually responded to the crisis with the Church Building Act of 1818, which set aside a large sum of money for the building of Anglican churches in the cities – too late to recapture the loyalty of the new working class, which had found inspiration and solace in the Nonconformist chapels, but not too late to perform one of the essential functions of the Anglican settlement, which is to re-enchant the view. For the Act coincided with the appearance of the first important manual of the Gothic style, Thomas Rickman's *Attempt to Discriminate the Styles of Architecture in England from the Conquest to the Reformation*. Rickman was, in fact, a Quaker. But his book justified the Gothic as the true English style, the style fit for an English church. Among Rickman's followers two stand out for their seriousness: Pugin and F. A. Paley (grandson of the Archdeacon, whose *Evidences of Christianity* held the floor until Darwin pulled away the carpet on which the Archdeacon stood). Both Pugin and Paley were convinced that 'God is in the details', and that a sacred architecture must be itself an act of consecration, in which holiness is inscribed in every line and shadow. This 'sacramental' concept of the Gothic is conveyed in Pugin's *True Principles of Christian Architecture*, and also in Paley's *Manual of Gothic Mouldings*, both published in 1841. Like Pugin, Paley converted to

Catholicism, influenced by the high church conception of architecture to go one higher still.

Pugin's love of the Gothic style began early, and led to an abhorrence of the Puritans who had destroyed so many beautiful things, in their sacrilegious war against what they took to be sacrilege. Recalling his spiritual journey in 1852, Pugin wrote:

I learned the truths of the Catholic religion in the crypts of the old cathedrals of Europe. I sought for these truths in the modern church of England, and found that since her separation from the centre of Catholic unity she had little truth, and no life; so, without being acquainted with a single Priest, through God's mercy, I resolved to enter his Church.[31]

By the time that was written, however, the Church of England had got the message. If Pugin could be converted by the Gothic style, then so could the heathen residents of England's towns and cities.

Ruskin, who took up the cause, was no fellow traveller of Rome, and sneered at Pugin for allowing himself 'to be stitched into a new creed by the gold threads on priests' petticoats'. His advocacy of the Gothic is certainly liturgical, but abounds in Puritanical appeals to purity, honesty and truth. His writings combine down-to-earthness with hieratic dignity, in the manner of the Book of Common Prayer, and he made the search for beauty in architecture coterminous with the search for salvation. 'When we build,' he wrote in *Seven Lamps of Architecture*, published in 1849, 'let us think that we build for ever.' And he meant this 'for ever' as much, and as little, as it is meant by those who pray in church, rounding off their words with 'for ever and ever, amen'. All buildings perish; and the Gothic Revival both accepts and denies this fact, raising symbols of for ever that may be as improvised and transient as a chapel in corrugated iron, or as rooted and immovable as Liverpool Cathedral – that last great creation of English architecture, by George Gilbert Scott, the man who also gave us the cast-iron telephone box, and whose grandfather had trained the architect of our church in Garsdon.

Ruskin was a fervent opponent of the Counter-Reformation and of everything in architecture that he deemed theatrical and false. He saw the Gothic Revival as a return to the natural piety of the medieval craftsman, whose work was offered as a gift to God. He yearned for an architecture in which the joining of stones would have the gentleness and firmness of the joining of hands in mar-riage. And he describes the Gothic style, in *Stones of Venice*, as a pure expression of the dignity of labour, in which the builder finds himself in his work. In short, his defence of the Gothic is expressed in low church concepts that would be equally congenial to the builder of a Nonconformist meeting house. Yet it was the orna-mental splendour of St Mark's, and 'the city of beautiful nonsense' whose Doge marries the sea, that most captured Ruskin's imagina-tion, and his defence of the Gothic, while uttered in low church accents, is really a plea for a sacramental architecture that would rise above the too abrupt and literal religion of the unornamented Word.

Very soon, of course, the Gothic style became a matter of

routine – as befits the official idiom of an established church. Sir George Gilbert Scott led the way, designing or altering some eight hundred buildings in his lifetime, and creating a kind of standardized Gothic that greatly offended the antiquarians of his day, leading many to accuse him of ruining the delicate medieval fabrics that he was in such demand to restore. Whether Garsdon has been ruined by Scott's former apprentice it is impossible to know, since there are no surviving records of the church's original nave and chancel. Our little church is like a thousand others scattered across the kingdom, recalling in all its machine-made Gothic parts the lost world of the medieval craftsman. And for all their perfunctory and mass-produced quality, these routine details endow Garsdon Church with its own quota of sacred mystery. Thanks to them you are aware, on entering, that this is not a meeting place but a shrine. Some of the high church yearning for the reserved sacrament, the votive offerings, the whispering confessional and the guttering candles before the favourite saint has been installed, in our church as in other churches across the kingdom, by an architecture that is consciously 'not of this world'. The loveliness of the Gothic mouldings so patiently anatomized by Paley; the intricacies of roll and fillet, edge and annulet, scroll and stiff leaf capital; the mystical cavities of piscina, aumbry, stoup and sepulchre; the wonders of tabernacle work and relief-encrusted spandrels – all such beauties have no place in the functional Gothic pattern-book used by Mr Coe at Garsdon. Nevertheless, the spirit that brought those wondrous details into being, and whose work still astounds us wherever the Puritans have left it intact – in our nearby church of

Fairford, for instance, as much as in Lincoln Cathedral – is the source whose last trickles our plain Gothic arches have captured and frozen.

Perhaps nothing is more surprising than the Englishness of the Gothic Revival. Pugin believed himself to be reviving the true architecture of the Roman Catholic faith, and rescuing it from the Protestant heresies that had flourished in England. But the style that he developed, and which was rapidly transported and bowdlerized around the globe, took root only in the English-speaking countries. In Pugin's day hardly a Gothic Revival church was built in Roman Catholic Europe – not because there was no need for new churches, but because the style seemed cold, expensive and irrelevant to the needs of ordinary believers. In England it marched across the landscape as the visible symbol of a new kind of evangelism – an evangelism of enchantment that was in stark and in some way dismissive contrast to the Wesleyan evangelism of faith. Its greatest monuments – from the Houses of Parliament to St Pancras Station, and from Lincoln College Chapel in Oxford to Liverpool Cathedral – are affirmations that this, where we are, is a Christian country, regardless of whether it is also a country of Christians.

While the architecture of our Church is marked by high church yearnings, the music that we sing has grown from the raw spirituality of low church believers. Like other Protestant Churches, the Church of England marked its departure from Rome by banning plainchant. John Merbecke composed a setting of Cranmer's first Prayer Book, using semi-rhythmical melodies partly derived from plainchant melisma. This setting became obsolete almost at once with the revision of the Prayer Book and was never replaced. It was revived in the nineteenth century, and an untouched copy of it used to lie by the organ in Garsdon Church. For a while, under Elizabeth I, Renaissance polyphony flourished, and – thanks in part to Queen Elizabeth's musicality – was allowed in churches. Byrd and Tallis wrote choral music to match that of Palestrina and Victoria; both remained loyal to the Roman Catholic Church, and both were soon disapproved and their music banned from sacred places. Although churches retained their choirs during the seventeenth century, they were permitted to enter the liturgy only with those grotesque metrical Psalms, monotonously chanted over limp chord progressions, which sound like nothing so much as slowed-down rap music uttered from the grave.

The people were soon impatient with that stuff, and at the end of the seventeenth century hymn singing began. Hymns remained officially illegal long after they had become a regular part of the Anglican service. The main sources were the Geneva Psalter – Calvin's permitted settings of the Psalms (including the Old Hundredth – 'All people that on earth do dwell' – along with others set by Louis Bourgeois) – a smattering of Luther's chorales, and the new collections of devotional hymns by Watts, Cowley, Newton and the Wesleys. In the open-air services of John Wesley, congregations were encouraged to affirm their faith in song, and the people took the songs into the official churches that they also attended, where often the choirs had for many years been silent. Although Wesley approved of singing, and published a book of hymns for two or three voices with bass continuo, he disapproved of the organ as 'the devil's instrument', and advocated a simple accompaniment on violin and viola da gamba.

Moreover, for the Nonconformists and Wesleyans who introduced hymn singing to the English churches, it was the words, and not the music, that principally mattered. The true pioneer was Isaac Watts (1674–1748), a Congregationalist of ecumenical views, who left some seven hundred and fifty hymns, many still in use today. His adaptation of Psalm 90 – 'O God, our help in ages past, / Our hope for years to come' – is still sung to the tune (St Anne) with which it was published in 1708, while another favourite, 'Jesus shall reign where'er the sun / Does his successive journeys run', acquired its most frequently used melody (Truro) in the *Psalmodia Evangelica*, published in 1789. Others, such as 'Come let us join our cheerful songs / With angels round the throne', are now set to nineteenth-century melodies. But their popularity derives less from the music, wonderfully suitable though it is, than from the clear and often inspiring verse. Until Watts, most religious songs were derived from the Psalms, and therefore had a decidedly Old Testament aura. Such indeed were the permitted hymns of the Geneva Psalter. Watts rescued the psalmody of the Congregationalists from Judaism and made it Christian. And the established church had no choice but to follow.

The nineteenth-century hymnals gradually drove out the angular tunes favoured by the Wesleys, and the poems too were adapted to Victorian taste. Isaac Watts's popular 'When I survey the wond'rous cross' retained its beautiful eighteenth-century melody; but it was often shorn of its fourth quatrain, redolent of

Counter-Reformation spirituality in the manner of St John of the Cross and St Teresa of Avila:

> His dying Crimson like a Robe
> Spreads o'er his Body on the Tree,
> Then am I dead to all the Globe,
> And all the Globe is dead to me.

Such sentiments lie a little beyond the border of Anglican piety – raw, devotional and inviting that physical identification with the sacrificial victim that is the pagan heart of the Roman Catholic liturgy.

Watts, Newton and the Wesleys were visionaries whose encounter with God was direct, unmediated, scarcely dependent on institutions or traditional forms. Charles Wesley was more visionary in his hymns than ever his brother was in his sermons, and if the English became Protestant under the Wesleyan influence it was not because of any change to the liturgy, but because their verses drew on the Bible rather than the Book of Common Prayer, and made the daily dedication of life more important than the half-yearly commemoration of the Eucharist. Here is an example:

> Jesus, the first and last,
> On thee my soul is cast:
> Thou didst the work begin
> By blotting out my sin;
> Thou wilt the root remove,
> And perfect me in love.

Yet when the work is done
The work is but begun:
Partaker of thy grace,
I long to see thy face;
The first I prove below,
The last I die to know.

Erik Routley has detected no fewer than eleven Biblical references in these lines, to Old Testament, Gospel and Epistle, all achieved by evoking words and phrases from the Authorized Version.[32] Charles Wesley could also be magnificently doctrinal, as in this famous condensation of the doctrine of the Incarnation:

Veiled in flesh the Godhead see,
Hail the incarnate Deity!
Pleased as man with man to dwell,
Jesus, our Immanuel...

Mild he lays his glory by,
Born that man no more may die;
Born to raise the sons of earth,
Born to give them second birth.

But this intrusion of abstract theology into English worship was accommodated and neutralized by singing. At Garsdon we belt out this famous hymn ('Hark, the herald angels sing') to the music of Mendelssohn, that gentle fellow traveller of the Christian faith whom Queen Victoria, then head of the Anglican Church, took to her heart, as the Church did also, despite the fact, and also because of the fact, that he was of Jewish extraction, grandson of the greatest of modern rabbis.

The hymnal shows us the extent to which the English Church has been not merely a religious institution, but the foundation of a genuine popular culture. Legal uncertainty meant that the official Anglican Church did not admit hymn singing into its services until the practice had become a thriving means of recruitment to the evangelical missions and, therefore, a threat to the Anglican supremacy. The first Anglican Church hymn book for general use was published in 1769, and included many of the Methodist and Congregationalist favourites. Charles Wesley's verses continued to be set to music, and his two sons – Charles and Samuel – were among the foremost composers of their day, though Samuel's conversion to Roman Catholicism led him to write Masses, motets and glees rather than straightforward hymn tunes. Samuel's illegitimate son and namesake, however, was a leading force in the choral movement that made the cathedral choir into one of the glories of Victorian England. His anthems and services, with their Romantic harmonies and poignant English melodies, epitomize the nostalgic vision of our country that lies at the heart of the Anglican faith, while his hymn tunes remain among the most memorable in the hymnal. There is surely little in the nineteenth-century hymnal to surpass his setting of 'The Church's one foundation / Is Jesus Christ her Lord' – a melody that cadences effortlessly in F minor, before returning to the home key of E-flat major.

Hymns passed freely from the Nonconformist to the established church and back again, so that by the middle of the nineteenth century the hymn was the living symbol of the English Churches, and of the unity-in-diversity that made them into a single and singular social force. In 1861 a group of Anglican clergymen gathered all the most popular hymns together in a unified collection, which was published as *Hymns Ancient and Modern*, and which at once became a national institution. Among English people of my generation only the tone deaf are without a repertoire drawn from this book, and from its semi-official successor, the *Anglican Hymn Book* of 1868. Like the Authorized Version of the Bible, the hymnal has helped to unite the Anglican and Nonconformist churches. The hymns have shaped the service of the Anglican Church, and made the congregation fully a part of it. They have replaced the Psalms as vehicles of collective sentiment, and the Psalms in their turn have become part of the liturgy.

In my youth the official *English Hymnal* had not yet taken over from *Hymns Ancient and Modern* either in churches or in schools. But the official hymnal gradually established itself, its appeal resting on the work of its greatest co-editor – Ralph Vaughan Williams – who had ensured that it contained both hymns that were older, and hymns that were younger, than those in the unofficial collections. As Vaughan Williams recognized, hymns are among the masterpieces of medieval monody, of Renaissance polyphony, and of German Renaissance and Baroque counterpoint. Few strophic songs achieve the melodic sublimity and harmonic intensity of the Passion Chorale, harmonized by Bach for the *St Matthew Passion*, and for a long time one of the most popular of Easter hymns. Fragments of plainsong have entered the hymnal – 'Pange Lingua', 'Veni Emmanuel'[33] – and several of Palestrina's hymns are also there. So too are the favourites from the Geneva Psalter, along with popular airs by Bach, Handel, Mendelssohn and Haydn. But the most important input has undeniably come from English composers themselves, and especially from the Romantics and proto-moderns.

A whole school of Victorian composers arose from the cathedral choir and its musical context, and the church choir, which was the foundation of musical education in England, helped to spread their music far and wide across the country. The very language of English Romanticism, from Parry and Stanford through Elgar, Holst and Vaughan Williams, to Ireland and Bax, is saturated with the idiom of the hymnal. Song and collective worship form the background to their music; and it is hardly surprising to discover that some of our most memorable hymns come from their pens. My own personal favourite – 'Come down O love divine', the translation of a fourteenth-century Italian poem – is set to a tune of Vaughan Williams, and named from the village, not far from Garsdon, where his father was vicar: Down Ampney. (The habit of naming hymn tunes after their place of origin dates from the late eighteenth century. Peruse the names of tunes in the *English Hymnal*, and you find yourself taken on a journey through rural England, knowing the spirit of each place from the melody that arose from it, and understanding, in another way, the inseparable connection between our Church and our country.)

Vaughan Williams died when I was already a lover of his music

– but a sceptical lover, who wondered whether such figures should not be put, like the rest of the old English enchantment, at the distance needed by the task of growing up. You could be a thoroughly modern person and still love *The Waste Land* and *Four Quartets*. You could, indeed you must, love Stravinsky, Schoenberg and Berg. Britten too was probably allowed. But surely not Vaughan Williams? Like Ruskin he was saturated with pastoral Christianity, and like Ruskin he lost his Christian faith while remaining a fellow traveller of the Church of England. Preoccupied to the end of his life by Shakespeare and Bunyan, he gave to *The Pilgrim's Progress* a serene and statuesque setting, more an oratorio than an opera, which stands as a monument to the English Church, both to its embarrassed ceremonial presence in the centre of national life, and to the low church fervour that it permitted and yet somehow managed to contain within unbreachable Gothic walls.

In a character like Vaughan Williams, indeed, we see the peculiar synthesis that the Anglican Church represents: belief and doubt, pomp and satire, a longing for the sacred combined with a sense that we create the sacred for ourselves – all this run together with a nostalgia for the lost England of Piers Plowman. It would be easy to dismiss the composer as a throwback, whose nineteenth-century harmonies and modal melodies belong to a transcended age. But there is a religious sentiment that runs through everything he composed, and which in some way unites it across the centuries with the first flowering, in the time of Elizabeth I, of our national church. If we lose that sentiment, then we lose our Church, and what remains will be spasms of evangelical fervour, in which the mass of ordinary, sceptical English people will have no part. The best of English religion is contained in the hymnal, and through the hymns English people hear the tread of those feet, in ancient times, on England's mountains green.

Such, at least, are the sentiments to which I incline, when leafing through the current *English Hymnal* behind my curtain, and seeing the name of Vaughan Williams on page after page. And there is another book too that the great man influenced – the *Oxford Book of Carols*, which dates from the thirties, and which is the record of a tradition that defines the one point where the English Church still enters the life of Everyman. Each European country has its repertoire of carols; but not every country makes Christmas into the central episode of the Christian faith. Nor was it always so in England. The Puritans took against Christmas, tried to ban it as a holiday, and the Pilgrim Fathers in Massachusetts succeeded for a while in erasing the feast from the calendar. But Christmas has a special significance in Northern countries, not only as the successor to the pagan festival of the winter solstice, but as the time when home and the comforts of home are iconized. For the English it is also the time when they can regain the protected house of childhood, and find the lamps of the old religion still shining on the walls.

Christmas is now the high festival of modern idolatry. But, hidden within the materialism and self-indulgence there remains an image of peace that has been woven together over two centuries, and which is conveyed in that quintessentially Anglican ceremony, the Festival of Nine Lessons and Carols. This service alternates texts from the King James Bible and carols adapted to the idiom of the festival choir, so as to tell the story of Christmas as the fulfilment of Old Testament Prophecy. It has no liturgical authority, and is a Victorian invention, devised by E. W. Benson (1829–96), then Bishop of Truro, later Archbishop of Canterbury, and a figure emblematic of Victorian Anglicanism, to whom I return in the chapter that follows.

Today the Festival is associated principally with King's College, Cambridge, an atheist establishment that pays the most beautiful lip service to a God in whom its Fellows (with a few odd exceptions) do not believe. Founded in the fifteenth century by King Henry VI, King's College is a microcosm of the English settlement, endorsed by both State and Church but belonging to neither, and evolving from Roman Catholic piety, through Reformation fervour to modern agnosticism without losing its sacramental aura or its disdain for the world. Only rarely is this aura made public, but at Christmas the chapel (one of the masterpieces of English Gothic) comes into its own, as a symbol of purity in a corrupted world, to the corruption of which its Fellowship has made its own eager contribution.

The invention of Christmas began in the eighteenth century, with Handel's *Messiah* setting passages from the King James Old Testament that Christians have always construed as prophecies of the coming Redeemer. The lovely words of the Book of Job – 'I Know that my Redeemer liveth, and that he shall stand at the latter day upon the earth' – are, in Handel's tranquil and heartfelt setting, the clearest statement of Christian hope that we English possess.

No reasoned argument could entitle us to affirm those words; but Handel's music lifts them out of the realm of argument and enables us, whatever the state of our faith, to identify with their message.

Handel founded the tradition of the English oratorio, which soon became the most popular of art forms, inspiring amateur choirs and instrumentalists across the country, and dominating the Three Choirs Festival, which has been held every year in one of the three cathedrals of Hereford, Gloucester and Worcester since the early eighteenth century. At my school we performed a yearly oratorio, and in Marlow town hall whoever wished could take part each Christmas in an amateur performance of the *Messiah*. This kind of choral singing was inseparable, in our feelings, from the Anglican religion: it was an assembly under the eyes of our God, in which Biblical words were sung to music that echoed their sacred meaning.

Those are only some of the thoughts that occupy me behind my curtain in this 'serious home on serious earth': thoughts at one remove from faith, in which I look upon the community, the nation and the history to which I belong through the illuminated window of the sacraments. Surrounded by high church architecture, pumping out low church hymns, I reflect on the long line of sceptical Englishmen, from Hobbes and Addison to Orwell and Larkin, for whom this strange form of holiness, which is really a prolonged falling short of holiness, has been the best that can be done in the matter of religion. The Anglican Communion is a form of sacramental religion in which all sorts and conditions of mankind are included, and in which anathemas and excommunications long ago ceased to have a point. And I rejoice that the Church to which I belong offers an antidote to every kind of utopian thinking. The Church of England is the Church of *somewhere*. It does not invoke some paradisal nowhere; nor does it summon the apocalyptic destruction of everywhere in the manner of the seventeenth-century Puritans.

Like Hobbes I remain attached to the idea of civil government and believe it to be superior in every way to the rule of priests. Life has taught me that civil government cannot exist without the nation and that a religion that conflicts with national sentiment will, like the Islam of the reactionary Salafists, destroy the hope of civil peace. Life has also taught me that a nation that strives to live without religion, in however muted and moderated a form, will never be able to call upon the loyalty of its citizens, and is destined to disappear. For three centuries we have enjoyed a dispensation in which religious and national sentiments endorsed each other, the first flowing into the gaps left by the second, and the second tempering the natural excesses of the first. That dispensation has gone, and what we celebrate in Garsdon is the memory of it.

So what happened to remove our Church from the central place that it once occupied in the national culture? Should we blame the loss of faith? Or the destruction of the liturgy? Or the vandalization of the English Bible? Or the social and cultural changes that have set everything in motion and put everything on sale? Or are there deeper causes, of which these changes are simply the superficial effects? In reflecting on these questions I shall try to say something about Christianity, and something about the post-Christian society in which the English now find themselves. I want to end this book with cheerful thoughts. But it will be for the reader to judge how cheerful they might be.

FOUR

Zeal Degree Zero

There are two kinds of god: those that emerge from a community, precipitated out, so to speak, from habits of association and attachment, and those that call a community into being. Pagan gods belong, on the whole, to the first kind. They reside in specific places, where comfortable shrines are made for them, and do little or nothing to disturb the moral order into which they are invited. They have human clothes, human faces and human passions, and when disregarded are apt to take a very human revenge. The Christian God belongs to the second kind. His infinite attributes and eternal being lie beyond human comprehension, and he communicates with his creatures in a timeless and placeless way for which we have no ready image except that provided by St John: he is the Word.

God spoke the world into being and then withdrew from it, to stand outside time, listening to the murmurs of human life, as we shape our feeble responses. Once, in his pity and exasperation at the sins of the world, God appeared among us, and gave his counsel directly. His life among us was also, as St Paul puts it (Philippians 2, 6–7), a self-emptying of his godhead, a continuous self-sacrifice ending in death. During his time on earth he established a new form of community, the Church, which was to endure to the end of time, endowed with his Holy Spirit, and to the membership of which we are called. How can this call be answered, while retaining our natural attachment to the place and time that are ours, and our necessary obedience to the laws of a temporal community?

In the Christian view the Jews had misunderstood the God who called to Moses from the burning bush and who later imposed upon him the sublime burden of the Commandments. They had assumed their God to be a god of the first kind – an ethnic deity, closely identified with the twelve tribes of Israel as they strove to wrest from their territorial competitors the space in which to settle down. But Christ came in part to tell them how wrong they were, that God looks on all his creatures with the same loving concern, and the same capacity to be offended at their sins. Muhammad relayed a similar message to the pagan tribes of Arabia, declaring that the God who spoke to them through the Koran was calling to all people everywhere, reminding them of a primeval allegiance and a universal law, of which God is the object and the source.

The Islamic *ummah* bears its name from a root meaning motherhood and source; it tells the Muslim that the nation to which he belongs is not of a time or a place, but of God. Wherever he is, the Muslim finds himself torn between a familial or tribal allegiance – a blood-bond that makes no real room for the stranger – and a call to a community that is not of this world, and which cannot be bound by any man-made law. Movements of revival within Islamic communities do not take the form of churches or councils, but declare

132

themselves as a form of 'brotherhood' – *ikhwân* – bound not by rules and procedures but by a visceral attachment that looks with suspicion on the outsider and the infidel.

Why did Christianity not go in that direction? Why did Christ's call to a universal membership not lead to the undermining of temporal authorities, and the destruction of the civil law? That Christ intended no such outcome is clear from the Gospels. But what did he do to prevent it? The answer is the Church. Christ did not issue a new set of commandments; he told his disciples only that they should love God entirely and their neighbour as themselves, something that they knew already from the Old Testament book of Leviticus. He left his disciples with an institution that they were to build in accordance with his example, and which would perpetuate his memory. Through that institution, he would always be present in their councils, and by agreeing with each other they would be agreeing with him.

At the core of the institution is the sacrifice – the once and eternal offering of God himself, as a propitiation for our sins. Through this sacrifice we enter another and higher community, which is not a community of this world, and is not in competition with secular authority. Its central sacrament celebrates the presence of God among us, through re-enacting his murder at our hands. No words can explain this sacrament, since sacraments are not explained but repeated. Their meaning belongs among the 'things which have been kept secret since the foundation of the world', to borrow the words of St Matthew's Gospel (13, 35).[34] Christ offered himself in a spirit of forgiveness, and in doing so made forgiveness into the gateway to salvation. We cannot understand this; but we can rehearse it, and in doing so enter into communion with his disciples, so as to be at one with others and with ourselves.

Put all the unresolvable metaphysical squabbles to one side, Hooker tells us, and then we shall see that the Eucharist is not the presence of Christ on the altar, as one object among others, but his presence in *ourselves*. Through the sacrament Christ 'imparteth himself even his whole entire Person *as a mystical Head* unto every soul that receiveth him, and that every such receiver doth thereby incorporate or unite himself unto Christ *as a mystical member of him*, yea of them also whom he acknowledgeth to be his own'.[35] It is this act of taking Christ inwardly into his being that transforms, refreshes and renews the Christian. And it is primarily in order to minister the sacraments that the Church exists. For it is thus that Christ lives in his disciples, and thus that the Holy Spirit animates their councils.

The sacraments mediate between man and God. They maintain spiritual order in the life of the individual and in the community. Hence a sacramental church can retreat from government, stay on the political sidelines, and allow communities to shape themselves according to a purely temporal obedience. That is how we should understand Pope Gelasius's doctrine of the 'two swords', mentioned in Chapter One. Nevertheless, however ingenious the separation, Church and State will intrude upon each other. The Church enjoins people to worship a single God, whose law is universally valid. How can conflict be avoided, between the local laws of the sovereign, and the universal laws of God? That question recurs again and again in the history of Christian communities, and throughout the seventeenth century the English struggled to find an answer to it. The answer is the Church of England: a church that unites a claim to apostolic authority with obedience to a temporal and territorial power.

This church has had both a spiritual and a temporal function. It is a vehicle for worship. And it is an endorsing presence in the life of the community, reinforcing the rites of passage on which social reproduction depends, and supporting the common moral code with authoritative words that do not melt away under the gaze of sarcasm but which remain staunch and tried and vigilant. Both those roles our Church inherited from the Church of Rome, and both have depended on its sacramental and apostolic character. Rites of passage are important: they are the vows that bind generation to generation across the chasm of our appetites. To think that politics can be conducted without reference to them, or that the institutions that endorse them can be left to look after themselves, is to live in cloud-cuckoo land.

In the early eighteenth century, when English society began to enjoy the fruits of civil peace, and the adventures of the colonists and the merchant seamen were beginning to bear fruit, the population of the country was largely rural, and the centres of religion and learning were as they had been in the days of *The Canterbury Tales* and *Piers Plowman*. Even today, the rural inheritance of the English Church is perpetuated in its diocesan structure. Its cathedrals are in old market towns. Canterbury was never a capital city, but merely a hub on the route between London and Dover. York had a certain importance in earlier times, but was bypassed by the Industrial Revolution and is of little economic significance today. Salisbury is a market town surrounded by the agricultural lands of the Salisbury Plain. Wells and Litchfield cathedrals are situated in small towns of which nothing now is ever heard.

Trollope's fictional Barchester illustrates the social and economic importance of the rural church, retained even in the mid-nineteenth century when Trollope wrote. For most of the eighteenth century the Anglican priesthood was settled in villages and market towns, in which the rectory was the most important residence after the manor. Emoluments and offices had not yet been brought under central administration, and the various livings, 'seats' and 'stalls' were in the gift of a motley collection of local squires, diocesan officials, cathedral chapter houses, distant colleges and even Parliament. I have already alluded to the abuses to which this gave rise. But not everything in this arrangement was bad: it contributed to the dispersal of power and authority that has, since the Glorious Revolution, curtailed the centralization of government in our country, and enabled local communities to address their problems without conceding a right of entry to the officers of the Crown. And it meant that men of education, ambition and culture would happily settle in a country rectory, and set a lamp of learning above their door.

Thus Oxford- and Cambridge-educated clergy were granted livings in every kind of out-of-the-way place, there to combine scholarly hobbies and pastoral care. We have the intimate portrait of one such clergyman in the records kept from 1758 until 1802 by the Rev. James Woodforde and published in 1924 as *The Diary of a Country Parson*. This kindly, worldly soul, who devoted as much attention to his table as to his clerical duties, conferred what energy was left on the education and relief of his poor parishioners, while enjoying his social status as one of the gentry. Woodforde's self-portrait has been filled out by Fielding, Goldsmith, Austen and others and nobody can doubt, from our present vantage point, that a rural rector in late eighteenth- and early nineteenth-century England was a secure and relatively comfortable pillar of society who nevertheless would frequently take his social duties seriously and devote his income to performing them. Such a clergyman was later invoked by Winthrop Mackworth Praed in his nostalgic poem 'The Vicar', written some time in the 1830s, describing the spontaneous hospitality and tolerant good nature of the Rev. Dr Browne:

> He wrote, too, in a quiet way,
> Small treatises, and smaller verses,
> And sage remarks on chalk and clay,
> And hints to noble lords and nurses;
> True histories of last year's ghost;
> Lines to a ringlet or a turban;
> And trifles to the Morning Post,
> And nothings for Sylvanus Urban...

The rural rectory was the home of eccentrics, amateurs, polymaths and bibliophiles. It also harboured some of the important scientific intellects of the time. The Rev. Stephen Hales was parish priest of

Teddington (then a village) when he began his experiments on plant and animal physiology, publishing his seminal *Statical Essays* between 1727 and 1733. The Rev. Thomas Robert Malthus was curate of the village of Okewood in Surrey in 1798 when he published the first volume of the world-changing *Essay on Population*. The Rev. Gilbert White was curate of Selborne in Hampshire when he wrote *The Natural History and Antiquities of Selborne*, which first appeared in 1789. This work, the fruit of a lifetime's observation, has been reprinted every year since then, and remains an authoritative account of the flora and fauna of the English countryside, before modern agribusiness began to lay waste to it.

Education was not compulsory for all children until late in the nineteenth century, when schools had already been provided by private foundations and the churches, and little remained for the State to do by way of capital investment. Such schools as existed in the eighteenth century were either established public schools and grammar schools or schools attached to an Anglican church. Fellows of the Oxford and Cambridge colleges were expected to be in Holy Orders, as were many schoolmasters, and it remained true until the mid-nineteenth century that Nonconformists could not attend the ancient universities – a disability that condemned the great hymnodist Isaac Watts to pursue his second career as a theologian and logician without the support of a community of scholars. In due course the Nonconformist churches established colleges and schools of their own, and it is arguable that the Anglican monopoly of the old universities and the public schools contributed thereby,

138

and against its design, to the expansion of educational opportunities during the eighteenth and nineteenth centuries.

The secure social position of the Anglican parson contributed to the perceived complacency of his Church, and to the latitudinarianism of many of its bishops. During the first part of the eighteenth century doctrine rapidly lost its importance, and the well-stocked libraries of the rural clergy would contain, along with the sermons of Joseph Butler, the writings of Enlightenment philosophers such as Locke and Montesquieu, as well as the novels of Richardson and Fielding, the poems of James Thomson and the growing literature of country sports. Although the Fellows of Oxford and Cambridge colleges were expected to be celibate, and remained so until the late nineteenth century, the rural parson was, if unmarried, an eligible bachelor and, as we know from Jane Austen, highly attractive to women of a certain class. In Trollope's *Barchester Towers* clergymen are both the subject and the object of powerful sexual emotions. With his secure social position, guaranteed income and hopes of preferment, the Anglican parson could ignore indigenous competition, and because he came into the narrow confines of the local community from some exotic elsewhere, bearing with him urban manners and the fruits of scholarship, he very quickly made conquests of the available hearts. Indeed, it may be thanks to the Anglican Church that the gene pool of rural England remained comparatively healthy during the years when its male population was losing its brighter members to the towns.

Yet, while the clergyman was a secure *pater familias* and a respected member of a rapidly modernizing society, the Church to which he belonged retained its medieval offices, its ancient cathedrals and their closes, and the collegiate domesticity that, thanks largely to Oxford and Cambridge, had survived the destruction of the monastic way of life. Preceptors, canons, prebendaries, chaplains and almoners; precentors, curates, deacons, wardens and deans; primates, bishops, suffragan bishops and archdeacons; chancellors, treasurers, vicars-choral, minor canons and canons-in-residence; reverends, very reverends, right reverends and graces… the endless list of offices and dignities endowed the clergy with an aura of a more ancient and slower-moving age, and gave to the idea of Holy Orders an antique resonance that it has not quite lost today.

Many institutions on which the English settlement rests acquired a connection to priestly offices in medieval times, and the Anglican Church has often inherited the connection. Thus – to take an institution close to my heart, since I am a member of it – the Inner Temple, which grew around the chapel of the crusading Knights Templar in the twelfth century, subsequently became home, following expropriation by Edward II, to a collegiate society of lawyers. Such societies – the Inns of Court – have, since the fifteenth century, exerted an officially sanctioned monopoly over the English bar. Although an autonomous institution without official ties to the State, the Temple, like the other Inns, is a fundamental part of the English political order: not a cornerstone, exactly, but a brick whose removal would lead to shifts and cracks across the whole surface of the building. The round church of the Templars was granted to the Inn in 1608, and the Master, who must be in Holy Orders, has been appointed by the Crown since the fifteenth century. Among the many distinguished Masters of the Temple Richard Hooker takes precedence, not only for what he was in himself, but also for the way in which he used this office, at the heart of the legal establishment, to bring peace to the warring factions of his day. The Temple church maintains a choir and an organist; and its services are the most beautiful of all those available in the City of London. And yet all around are the chambers of worldly and ambitious lawyers, most of whom are never seen in their church.

Almost all the educational, legal and governmental structures that came down from the Middle Ages retained their connection to Holy Orders after the break with Rome, and the Anglican Church emerged from the seventeenth-century turmoil in possession of these social privileges. During the eighteenth century the career of clergyman reached into academic, legal and administrative offices, endowing those offices with an aura of holiness and the priestly vocation with a residue of worldly power. The titles of the Church belong with the Gothic Revival buildings, with the chasubles and surplices, robes and vestments, with aumbry, credence table, Galilee and rood loft – features that lack any worldly explanation and which, therefore, lifted churches, colleges and the offices of learning and law out of empirical reality into a transcendental nowhere. Never has a Christian clergyman been more comfortably in this world than in eighteenth-century England; and seldom has his position been embellished with so many reminders that he is nevertheless not *of* this world.

It scarcely needs saying that such a situation could not last. The revival movement of John Wesley and George Whitefield set a standard to which the Church could not quickly adapt. By the end of the century Wesleyism had ceased to be a revival *within* the Church and become a rival *to* it. The migration of the rural work-force to the towns deprived the rural vicar of much of his congregation, and the evangelizing zeal of the Wesleyans began to discredit the formal services of the established church. Arriving in the manufacturing towns, the new workers either drifted away from religious observance or, if they sought for a place of worship, were more likely to find a Nonconformist meeting house than one of the sparsely scattered Anglican churches. Wesley himself showed no tendency to political radicalism, ending his life as he had begun it, a settled Tory. And the Nonconformist chapels were as much the cradles of the new forms of middle-class respectability as of social radicalism. It was only with the arrival of the Primitive Methodists, who started building their chapels in 1811, and who made a con-scious effort to evangelize the urban working class, that Methodism became a serious voice within the trade union and socialist move-ments. Nevertheless, it is clear in retrospect that the Anglican Church found itself at the end of the eighteenth century in a false position in relation to the economic, demographic and political upheavals that were changing the face of England.

On the other hand, not all rural parsons were formed on the Trollopian model. Charles Kingsley (1819–75), taking up his post as rector of Eversley in Hampshire in 1844, noted that his parishioners came rarely to church, took Communion at most once a year, and had little or no knowledge of the Bible or the Prayer Book. He set about rectifying this dereliction, and thereby became the most

famous country parson of the nineteenth century. Kingsley illustrates the enormous transformation that then came about, as the
Anglican Church attempted in its own way to address the ills of the
new industrial society, while holding on to its privileged position as
the spiritual wing of government. Kingsley was an active supporter
of the Chartists, a co-founder of the Christian Socialist Movement
and author of the popular children's classic *The Water Babies*
(1863), memorably dramatizing the case against child labour. He
was also a traditional country parson, a lover of field sports (especially hunting and fishing) and a child of the British Empire, whose
descriptions of the North African desert (in *Hypatia*, 1853) and the
South American wilderness (in *Westward Ho!*, 1855) are replete with
colonial nostalgia and a belief in the privilege of being English in a
world where most people lack such a stroke of good luck.

By the time Kingsley was writing, the Christian religion had
received a series of intellectual shocks that made the childlike faith
of a Henry Vaughan, an Isaac Watts or a Charles Wesley no longer
available to an educated clergyman. The arguments of Hume and
Kant had undermined the claims of rational theology, and Biblical
scholarship had demoted Holy Scripture from the Word of God to
words inspired by God. Kingsley was *au fait* with these develop-
ments and also with the science of his day, being one of the first
churchmen to welcome Darwin's *Origin of Species* (1859). He did
not see the theory of evolution as a threat to Anglican Christianity,
which was, as he saw it, a truth-directed faith, open to argument and
to the investigation of nature. On the other hand, there were forms
of the Christian faith that verged on superstition, which sought for

a world full of magic and mystery, and these were the true enemies of Christ. Kingsley saw superstition as the permanent threat to the Christian philosophy that had triumphed at the Reformation. Superstition could wear a Christian face, just as truth could appear in the garments of philosophy. In *Hypatia* he did justice at last to a woman, one of the last pagan philosophers, who had been brutally murdered by a Christian mob in fifth-century Alexandria, and who in Kingsley's eyes was as much a martyr to the truth as those burned at the stake by Mary Tudor. Superstition, he believed, was still rife, and its principal protector in the Christian world was the Roman Catholic Church. And it was in mocking John Henry Newman's conversion to Rome that Kingsley came out most strongly as a defender of the Anglican settlement.

Newman (1801–90) was a leader of the Oxford Movement, so called because its most prominent members – John Keble, Newman and Edward Bouverie Pusey – were ordained clergy attached to Oxford colleges, and hence committed (for the time being at least) to celibacy. The Oxford Movement began in the 1830s, as a reaction against the low church approach to the liturgy that had come about under the influence of Wesleyism and the Nonconformist churches. Newman and Pusey issued a series of brilliantly written 'Tracts for the Times', in which they argued for a return to high church traditions, and a recognition of the historical and apostolic connection between the three 'branches', as they called them, of the Catholic Church – the Roman, the Orthodox and the Anglican. They emphasized the sacramental character of the Christian tradition, and the need to bring the mystery of Christ's presence into the lives of ordinary people – something that could not be done, they believed, by utilitarian sermons and shopkeeper morality, but which required the full panoply of liturgical invocation, such as the Church had, in its higher moments, sought to provide. Newman converted to Roman Catholicism, and in reply to Kingsley's satirical assault, published his *Apologia pro vita sua* (1865–6), which remains one of the classics of confessional literature. Now beatified by Pope Benedict XVI, Cardinal Newman, as he became, stands as a reminder of the thin line that divides high church Anglicanism from the Roman alternative.

The scandal of the Oxford Movement occurred in the wake of the Catholic Relief Act of 1829. This removed the remaining disabilities that had prevented the Roman Catholic Church from functioning in Britain, and led Coleridge to compose his important essay *On the Constitution of Church and State* (1830). In defending a national church Coleridge found himself arguing that the religion of such a church is less important than its loyalty. He identified the principal enemy of the national church as priestly celibacy, combined with attachment to a power outside the kingdom. A married priest, he believed, acquires an attachment to the people of the country in which he practises. The celibate priest is free to identify his affections and loyalties outside the temporal order and can, therefore, be manipulated by those who claim to represent some higher and more godly power than those who maintain the secular state.

Quaint though this discussion may seem to people in our sexualized age, it nevertheless touches on a matter that goes to the heart of the Church's position in our society today. Newman opted for the Roman Catholic Church partly because it phrased its mission as a renunciation of this world. Chastity, he believed, lifts priesthood out of the flow of worldly events and endows it with the character of a sacrament. The Catholic priest is a symbol of spiritual purity, and through the Mass he evokes the transfigured world that Christians can enter only when they have cast off the flesh entirely.

Newman was not the only member of the Oxford Movement who converted. The legalized Roman Catholic Church offered a glowing exit sign to those whose need for mystery and ritual turned them against the disenchanted world that was growing around them. A kind of Roman Catholic Renaissance occurred during the nineteenth and early twentieth centuries, and included among its distinguished converts the historian and satirist Ronald Knox,[36] the poet Gerard Manley Hopkins (who became a Jesuit priest), the architect Augustus Pugin, and even one of the sons of the Archbishop of Canterbury, Robert Hugh Benson, whose conversion, and promotion to the rank of monsignor, profoundly shook the Anglican establishment – an episode to which I return below.

It should not be thought that this move towards Roman Catholicism was simply an escapist response to the social problems that troubled Kingsley. Bishops refused to give livings to Tractarians, as the followers of the Oxford Movement were called. Many such, therefore, ended up working in the industrial slums. Their experience led to the foundation of the Christian Social Union, devoted to remedying the lot of the poor, and including several bishops among its members. Nor was the Anglo-Catholic emphasis on liturgy and the celebration of the Eucharist without a wider effect on our Church. On the contrary, the Oxford Movement influenced the practice of the whole Church in a sacramental direction, and in the conflict between the Wesleyan and the Tractarian tendency it is hard, now, to assign victory to either side. It was not the cathedral aristocracy or the upper echelons of the Anglican priesthood that responded to the call for a more holy, mysterious and sacramental form of worship. The first surpliced choir appeared in Leeds parish church, and by the end of the nineteenth century, when (following the 1870 Act) education had become compulsory and the villages were full of boys who could read, robed choirs and processions, chants and sung liturgies were common all across the kingdom.

John Wesley and John Henry Newman were the two greatest apostles of Christ that the Church of England has produced, and it could contain neither of them. But it is a measure of its ecumenical strength that the Church nevertheless survived both the Nonconformist onslaught in the industrial towns, and the rise of the Oxford Movement, and that all the changes that resulted were resolved without undermining the legal privileges of Anglicanism or its place in the unwritten constitution of the kingdom. In one respect things continued as normal, with the Anglican Church maintaining its central place in the system of schools and colleges, in Parliament and the military, and in all the ceremonies in which the monarchy and its honours were at stake. But insensibly the identity between the Anglican Church and England was being eroded. The imperial expansion naturally led to the import of the official church to those places, such as Canada and Australia, in which the colonial population was dominant. Moreover, an Episcopal church, offshoot of the Elizabethan and Jacobean settlement, had been established in Scotland, and had extended its reach to the United States of America.

The movement to evangelize native populations was not born from the Anglican Communion. Although a Society for the Propagation of the Gospel in Foreign Parts had been established within the Anglican Church in 1701, it was directed at the spiritual needs of the colonists rather than at those of the native populations, who at the time were assumed to be more likely to eat missionaries than to learn from them. Indeed, the Society existed to safeguard the English identity of the colonists, rather than to propagate the faith. The real missionary movement took off much later, inspired in part by *The Rise and Progress of Religion in the Soul* (1749), a work by the Nonconformist leader, Philip Doddridge, some of whose hymns have found their way into the *English Hymnal*. And the most important figure in the movement, William Carey, was a Baptist.

By the time the Anglican Church joined in, the Methodists, Baptists, Congregationalists and Unitarians were well installed across the Empire. Nevertheless, Anglican missions began to flourish during the course of the nineteenth century, and by the end of the century the King James Bible, the Book of Common Prayer and *Hymns Ancient and Modern* formed a lingua franca of Christian worship all around the globe. By that time the Church of England was no more English than the Church of Rome was Roman. Its most important controversies today – those over women priests and homosexuality – are being fought out between American liberals and African conservatives, with the old English establishment looking on in mild astonishment at the fuss.

Trollope's vision of the nineteenth-century Church of England, as a career path within the English class system, closely connected to the path of politics, has the ring of truth. Describing the rector of the village in which she was raised in the 1860s, the composer Ethel Smyth wrote that:

> he was not, and did not pretend to be, a strenuous priest, but simply an incumbent of the old school – that is a man of good family and education, who looked upon his rectorship as a sinecure, and would have considered special attention to the morals and spiritual needs of his flock eccentric and rather impertinent.[37]

But that 'old school' was not, even then, the only school. The battle against slavery and child-labour and the campaigns for a nation-wide system of education and healthcare occupied many within the Anglican Church besides Charles Kingsley, and the Christian Socialist movement flourished after 1848, publishing a series of Tracts on Christian Socialism devoted to rewriting the Gospel as a rebuke to the property-owning class.

The YMCA, founded in 1844 to cater for the lonely young men who had flocked to the cities, was the inspiration of George Williams, a young draper who helped to bring the Church into the centre of a worldwide ecumenical movement for the

Christianization of the industrial cities. By the end of the nineteenth century, when the Trollopian E. W. Benson was succeeded by the liberal Frederick Temple as Archbishop of Canterbury, the Church of England was taking the lead in educational reform and social advocacy. Temple's son William, who became Archbishop of Canterbury from 1942 until his death in 1944, was president of the Workers' Education Association, and led a movement to align the Church of England with socialist ideas of justice. His close friend R. H. Tawney, arguably the most influential lay Anglican of the twentieth century, published the three books that were to wean the Anglican hierarchy away from its old complacency: *The Acquisitive Society* (1921), *Religion and the Rise of Capitalism* (1926) and *Equality* (1931). Archbishop Temple's own literary contribution, *Christianity and Social Order* (1942), set out the agenda for a new and mildly socialist church that would use its established position to work for the legislation required by the Welfare State. While it may have been true at the end of the nineteenth century to describe the Anglican Church as the Tory Party at prayer, it would be more correct to say, of its leaders today, that they represent the Labour Party trying to remember how to pray, while not really understanding the point of it.

More disturbing than the social upheavals of the nineteenth century were the scientific advances in biology and anthropology, which were rapidly putting in question the idea of humanity as the summit of creation. Under the influence of Darwin and of the secular morality of the Utilitarians, educated people began to doubt both the truth of the Church's teaching and the need for its help. A kind of humanist agnosticism spread through the educated classes, leading Matthew Arnold to write his famous poem 'On Dover Beach':

> The Sea of Faith
> Was once, too, at the full, and round earth's shore
> Lay like the folds of a bright girdle furled.
> But now I only hear
> Its melancholy, long, withdrawing roar,
> Retreating, to the breath
> Of the night-wind, down the vast edges drear
> And naked shingles of the world.

Arnold was son of Thomas Arnold, headmaster of Rugby School, whose advocacy of 'muscular Christianity' inaugurated the curriculum reforms that created the Victorian public school. Matthew's defence of high culture, in *Culture and Anarchy* (1867–8), could be read as an attempt to graft the Anglican inheritance on to another root than the root of faith – one immune to the phylloxera of scientific knowledge. Arnold was not alone in this attempt. Many of the greatest English minds of the nineteenth century took a share of it: John Ruskin, Walter Pater, George Eliot, and many more. It didn't entirely work. But it is undeniable that English literature since that time has been dominated by writers who defend a sacramental vision of England as part of our cultural legacy, and therefore as something that can go on flourishing, even if no longer rooted in faith.

That is surely the view that comes across from the poems and the Wessex novels of Thomas Hardy, from Conrad's vision of the English Merchant Navy and its residue of imperial virtue, from the Anglican pilgrimage of T. S. Eliot, even from the agnostic sense of loss in Orwell and Larkin. And in the criticism of F. R. Leavis this desire for culture as a 'real presence' that will provide the Eucharistic moments in the life of our nation becomes all but explicit – and with a pronounced low church accent, identifying Bunyan and Blake as the leading figures in a tradition of creative dissent. It is only because of the Church of England that this view of English culture has been possible, and it is this very view of English culture that drew me, aged fifteen, into the Anglican Church, not knowing how much I should have to believe in order to claim the Church's comforts.

In the world of Jane Austen sexual feelings are an acknowledged part of life, to be domesticated and subdued by marriage. Matrimony is the rite of passage for which both men and women prepare themselves, and clergymen take their place in the queue like everyone else, distinguished from other men, if at all, only by their greater capacity to see the thing through. In the course of the nineteenth century, however, the English discovered sex as something distinct from love, marriage and reproduction. The discovery was so dreadful that neither the Church nor its opponents could admit that it had happened. Women had to be rescued from this monstrous disease, and placed in a permanent quarantine. Lewis Carroll remade the English female as a pre-pubescent girl, whose wisdom dismisses and destroys the adult world. The sexuality of Dickens's heroines is an untouchable secret. Ruskin notoriously turned from his bride at the sight of her naked body, and, while the Pre-Raphaelites had their fair share of romps, the image of woman that they made iconic was of a withdrawn and spectral creature, a water nymph who would dissolve into a crystalline puddle at the first human touch.

The Anglican Church sought to avoid the turmoil caused by sex, not least on account of the Church's dominant presence in the all-male public schools and in the all-male Oxford and Cambridge colleges, whose Fellows were bound to celibacy. The eighteenth-century domestication of sex had somehow enabled people to live with these survivals from the monastic era. A college or a school was simply another form of domesticity, and sexual urges, should they occur in such places, could be released on the playing field, or buried in books.

At the time the English public school and the Anglican Church were the pillars of the old English establishment, and they leaned on each other for support. 'Public school' means a particular kind of private school, usually established in the later Middle Ages, and originally designed to offer education to poor scholars, funding itself from its richer clientele and from charitable donations. The public schools entered a new phase with the arrival in 1828 of the above-mentioned Dr Arnold, the vigorous evangelical Christian headmaster of Rugby, who endowed that particular school with what was soon to become its famous ethos celebrated uncritically in the popular novel *Tom Brown's Schooldays*.[38] Teaching was reformed, with a strong emphasis on Greek and Latin, mathematics obtained

its central place in the curriculum, and athletics was made fundamental to the whole course of a pupil's study, on the principle of
mens sana in corpore sano. Most pupils boarded at the school and
were, therefore, from an early age (twelve onwards) kept at a
distance from home throughout the term, in the company of other
boys and the masters. Few girls were ever encountered, and women
too were in short supply. The absence of female company, the presence of pre-pubescent and post-pubescent boys in intimate contact,
and the intoxicating mixture of athletics and Hellenism, with Plato
and Theocritus singled out for special attention, could not but exert
a suggestive influence on the boys. And the quarantining of female
sexuality meant that women were divided, in the thinking of Victorian schoolboys, into two classes: virgins and whores, both forbidden.

It always astonishes me to discover people who think that religion and sex have nothing to do with one another, and that you can
act as you like in the one sphere while thinking what you should in
the other. In fact, of all the rites of passage that religions have taken
under their wing, that of sexual initiation has been by far the most
tenaciously adhered to. English people today look with incredulity
on the habit in some Muslim communities of veiling and hiding
women, of forcing them to marry the man chosen for them, and of
occasionally killing them for 'honour's' sake. What can this possibly
have to do with obedience to Allah, the compassionate, the merci-
ful, they ask themselves? In fact, it has everything to do with it. Sex
is not only the gateway through which the next generation enters
the community; it is the place in which our actions are most un-
avoidably subject to the ethic of 'pollution and taboo'.

Medieval writers such as Chaucer, Dante and Petrarch, taking their inspiration from Plato, represented erotic love as a sacred bond, an aspiration to the highest purity, and a transcendence of the body and its appetites. And when the Church declared marriage to be a sacrament it was in response to similar ideas. Right down to modern times the sacramental nature of the sexual act has been acknowledged in art and literature, even in the literature of transgression, which has seen what Georges Bataille called '*l'érotisme*' as a way of acknowledging the sanctity of the individual, while at the same time opening the way to violation.[39]

The connection between sex and the sacred is the theme for another book, and since I have written that book I shall leave the topic to one side.[40] Nevertheless, it seems to me that the evolution of the Anglican Church cannot be understood independently of the Victorian mystification of women and the subsequent desanctifying of the sexual act. The institutional commingling of the public schools and the old universities with the Church, with the hierarchy of appointments moving freely between the three, meant that there was no truly independent spiritual force that stood in judgement over the education of the young. Hence there evolved in England a kind of education that, although ostensibly dedicated to the production of upright Christian gentlemen, who would administer the Empire on behalf of the Queen, and who would marry and bear children for their country's sake, was in many ways close to the *paideia* of the Greeks – except that it seems to have lacked the disciplined nature of the man–boy relationship as this was maintained (according to Jaeger's great study) in ancient Greece.[41]

The artistic and literary culture of England was intimately connected with the public schools and with the Anglican Church right up until the Second World War. Dr Arnold produced two literary sons, besides Matthew. His granddaughter was Mrs Humphry Ward, the novelist, whose works portray the spiritual conflicts through which the descendants of Dr Arnold lived – between high and low church, between Roman and Anglican Catholicism, between Biblical doctrine and Biblical scholarship and, underlying them all, the ever-growing conflict between religion and science. In *Helbeck of Bannisdale* (1898) Mary Ward (as she is now remembered) tells the story of love, hate and sexual passion between a Roman Catholic, head of an old recusant family, whose dark spirituality has been nurtured on forbidden mysteries, and the daughter of a Cambridge atheist, who is torn between awe and mockery in the presence of sacramental rites, and who is eventually driven to suicide. This disturbing story shows sex and religion fighting for the human soul, and Ward is clear that you cannot obey the one force without provoking the other.

Dr Arnold's daughter married into the Huxley family, so linking the Arnolds to the Darwinians. Dr Arnold was singled out by Lytton Strachey, the mischievous historian, as one of his 'Eminent Victorians', whom it was important to debunk, since he represented, like the other victims chosen by Strachey, a kind of stiff and patriotic code of honour that was at variance with the moral anarchy that Strachey discerned (and wanted to discern) just below the surface of Victorian England.[42]

Lytton Strachey, the son of a distinguished general, spent some time as a graduate student at Trinity College, Cambridge, where he was a member of 'the Apostles', a secret society founded in 1820. At the time of his membership the Apostles regarded themselves as inhabiting a higher ethical sphere from that occupied by ordinary patriotic Englishmen.[43] They were a kind of anti-matter to the Anglican substance. Other members included the philosophers G. E. Moore and Bertrand Russell and the mathematician and economist John Maynard Keynes. They subsequently formed the nucleus of the Bloomsbury Group, centred on Bloomsbury Square in London – a loose association of upper-class bohemians, who managed to be simultaneously an establishment and the scourge of all establishments. For the Apostles sexuality was no longer the 'guilty secret' of the Victorians. They were heirs to the fin-de-siècle, had absorbed the lessons of Oscar Wilde's *Salomé* and the extraordinary apology for polymorphous sexuality written by Havelock Ellis and John Addington Symonds. This book, *Sexual Inversion*, published in 1897, was followed by Havelock Ellis's *Studies in the Psychology of Sex*, which began appearing in the same year. After such works sex was out in the open, and – the trial of Oscar Wilde notwithstanding – Christian marriage and the heterosexual worldview upon which it depended began rapidly to lose their social status.

No figure was more emblematic of late Victorian intellectual life than E. W. Benson, who pursued an ecclesiastical career that brought him to the notice of Queen Victoria, and who became headmaster of Wellington College, a public school founded by the Prince Consort and therefore (following the Prince's untimely death) dear to the Queen's grieving heart. Benson had been educated at King Edward's School in Birmingham, under a headmaster influenced by Dr Arnold, and was vehemently attached to the 'muscular Christianity' idea. He married a woman, daughter of the philosopher Henry Sidgwick, to whom he had proposed when she was a child sitting on his knee, and who never could conform her life to his rigid principles. Indeed, there is some evidence that Mrs Benson compensated for her passionless marriage with chaste but passionate attachments to other women.[44] She was a close friend in later life of Ethel Smyth, who, with the novelist Radcliffe Hall (author of *The Well of Loneliness*), was one of the first public lesbians in English culture.

Mrs Benson bore four sons and two daughters to E. W. Benson, and the three surviving sons became significant figures in turn-of-the-century culture. By the time the sons were going through Cambridge, after their years in public school, their father had become, first, Bishop of Truro, and then Archbishop of Canterbury, moving in the highest political and intellectual circles. The three sons seem to me to epitomize the 'trivium' that faced the educated members of the English establishment during the run-up to the First World War. They could go in one of three directions. They could take the old imperial idea as their motto, even marry a lady of 'good breeding stock', and maybe pay with their life in the coming disaster, leading from the front with the fervour of doomed youth. Or they could join the flippant and cynical culture that was beginning to emerge around people like Lytton Strachey, Aubrey Beardsley and Oscar Wilde, seeing it rather as a justified rebuke to the stiff and de-sexed certainties of Victorian England. Or they could turn away, in search of another and more genuine form of spirituality than was offered by the Anglican Church (which was, for intellectuals of that generation, too much embroiled in the imperial project to be credible as doctrine, and too quaint in its manners to be of any more than theatrical appeal).

Those three paths were separately taken by the Archbishop's three surviving sons. Thus the first of them, A. C. Benson, became a master at Eton, a Cambridge don, and a famous author of Christian essays and verse, imbued with a stiff patriotic melancholy. It is to him that we owe the words of our unofficial national anthem, 'Land of Hope and Glory', sung to the trio section of Elgar's 'Pomp and Circumstance March' no. 1. (Note, however, that Elgar was a Roman Catholic, whose feelings for England intensified as his faith declined.) Like his father, the Archbishop, and his unfortunate sister, A. C. Benson suffered from some kind of bipolar disorder, rendering him prone to fits of deep depression – fits that were in some way authenticated by his gentle and melancholic essays.

The second surviving son, E. F. Benson, was a fashionable novelist, extremely successful in his day with the stories of Mapp and Lucia. He wrote fascinating memoirs of his life and times – *As We Were* (1930) and *As We Are* (1932), plotting the radical change in the English psyche as a result of the Great War. In 1914 he published the story of David Blaize, set in an imaginary English public school, in which the topic of sexual passion between older and younger boys is openly explored, though in ways that condemn any overt physical expression. *David Blaize* had a sensational impact, and E. F. Benson received letters from soldiers at the front thanking him for this book that consoled them with the idealized vision of their school days and the pure loves that they had then enjoyed. Its sickly sentimentality and shallow prose are more noticeable today than its erotic undercurrents; but it was followed at the time by more David Blaize novels by Benson, and was not thought to be in the slightest corrupting – on the contrary its message was one of boy-scout purity. (Note that the period also saw the birth of the Scout movement under Baden-Powell.) The lesson that we might draw from E. F. Benson is that the flippant culture to which Wilde belonged was entirely contiguous with the dignified patriotic Anglicanism of Benson's father and older brother, and represented a clear option for members of the upper class who could not go along with the stuffy certainties that were about to be blown away by the First World War.[45]

Finally, there was the youngest brother, Hugh Benson, who entered the Anglican Church only to find himself longing for a more universal and more apostolic form of spirituality, and eventually turning his back on the whole Anglican settlement in which he had been bred, to embrace the Church of Rome. He lived much of his time in Rome, rising to the rank of monsignor, and was much fêted by the Roman Catholic establishment – after all, to have converted a son of the Archbishop of Canterbury represented a radical inroad into the Protestant citadel. He was also a noteworthy writer, with serious devotional works as well as children's books, science fiction and visionary plays to his credit.

It seems to me that this trivium continued to define the existential choice of the privileged class in England after the First World War. The Bensons brilliantly illustrate its reality, since they were all three offspring of the highest representative of the unified Anglican culture – the Archbishop of Canterbury himself. The war swept away the certainties, such as they were, of the Anglican settlement, but left this trivium in place. The question was still: do we go forward along the old Anglican path, the path of patriotic loyalty and dignified churchgoing; do we sink into the world of sensual gratification and facetiousness; or do we turn our backs on the whole thing, and seek repose in some other, more universal, more eternally rooted faith?

That was the question confronted by the new generation of public school boys, who were at school during the Great War, and young men shortly thereafter, and it was a question predicated upon leisure. Only members of a privileged class could have that kind of existential choice. For other, more normally situated people, the questions of how to earn a living, how to make one's way in the world, how to achieve security, ensured that allegiances and ideals could not be chosen, but must be accepted as the common destiny of those whose first goal is survival. Such people, if Christian at all, would most likely have been Nonconformist. And they would have formed, in the eyes of Bloomsbury, the despised foundation of society, the 'marrying classes', for whom patriotism is a *sine qua non* and a sign of submission to fate. Ordinary people would have reacted with abhorrence to E. M. Forster's expression of the Bloomsbury worldview: 'if I had to choose between betraying my country and betraying my friend, I hope I should have the guts to betray my country.'[46] But it was ordinary people whose national loyalty was to be called upon, when Britain was dragged into another war, and when many of the intellectuals chose to betray them, whether or not for the sake of a friend.

Among the most important representatives, from the cultural point of view, of the privileged elite were the novelist Christopher Isherwood and the poet W. H. Auden, who collaborated on various projects, including the play *The Ascent of F6*. Isherwood and Auden's literary apprenticeship occurred during the years following the First World War and culminating in the Depression. The first path of the trivium – that of the English-Anglican idyll – had been sown with brambles by the war and few artists still trod it. Those who did – the poet Walter de la Mare, the composer Ralph Vaughan Williams, painters like the Nash brothers, and those last exponents of the classical idea in architecture, Lutyens, Belcher and Curtis Green – were despised by the new class of modernist intellectuals. On the other hand, during the Second World War that was soon to follow, the country leaned upon these exponents of the English idea (to whom Churchill belonged by temperament), since the modernists had nothing to offer a people fighting for survival and in need of an icon of their homeland.

Auden was descended on both his father's and mother's side from Anglican clergymen, and his Anglican faith was to return in later life, when he joined the movement of Anglo-Catholic sentiment and, in his own peculiar way, looked for the first path of the trivium. However, the intellectuals around Auden had been raised in a weakened Anglican faith, or in no faith at all. Their time at

Cambridge or Oxford was devoted to cynical amusements. And they had turned their backs on the upper class values that had been impressed upon them (though somewhat feebly) at public school. They were ripe for the great 'conversion experience'. Few of them went the way of Hugh Benson, into the arms of the Catholic Church. For many of them the redeeming, universal faith that would rescue them from the old worn-out platitudes of an unbelievable patriotism was that propagated by the Communist Party. And because they contained, in their souls, a certain visceral hatred towards the society in which they had been raised, and a contempt for its stiff, corseted principles, their attachment to communism went further than belief, and spilled over into action. They conceived the desire to 'join' the movement, and thereby to live out their fantasies of aggression towards the world into which they had been born.

As we all know, a particular group of them – Kim Philby, Guy Burgess, Donald Maclean and Anthony Blunt – formed at Cambridge (where at least two of them were Apostles) the circle that was to penetrate, under instructions from the Comintern, the Foreign Office and secret service, before, during and after the Second World War. Their work for the Comintern was immensely damaging, but caused them no apparent remorse, even though they betrayed many people to their deaths, and ensured that Stalin would be able to advance as far as possible into Eastern Europe. Auden knew them, referred to them dismissively as the 'homintern', and, after a brief flirtation, entirely rejected the worldview that they served.

Those artists and intellectuals who rose above the orgiastic nihilism that gripped the English educated classes at that time – Auden and Britten pre-eminently – did so through a rediscovered Anglican spirituality, itself the result of intense artistic labour. Those who had fled into the arms of the Communist Party often had only one fixed point in their attitude to others, which was the desire to betray them. Treachery became an end in itself, the final justification of an otherwise destructive life, and the proof of their attachment to a universal and redeeming cause. This sounds odd, perhaps, but it is not so odd, if you think of the commitment to communism as arising from a gesture of repudiation, wilfully misunderstood as the pursuit of an ideal.

In a public school like Eton, Anglicanism was a strong presence, and Cyril Connolly describes, in his autobiographical account of the school in the post-First World War period, a fierce contest in many of the boys between sexual passions and religious scruples, often experienced as a conflict between 'romance' and 'character', the latter being an all-embracing name for the imperial virtues.[47] However, it is important to remember the peculiar nature of the English Church, both in the imperial version that was part of the spiritual hardware of the public schools, and in the more mystical 'Anglo-Catholic' version that appealed to Eliot, Auden and Britten.[48] The return to Christianity was envisaged by the Second World War generation as a return to England and Englishness, a rediscovery of essentially *earthly* roots, the recognition, in Eliot's words, that 'history is now and England'.

Auden's return to Anglicanism was a private accomplishment of his own, as were Eliot's and Britten's, and was regarded with ironical compassion by his atheist contemporaries. It occurred while Auden was in America, homesick and guilty towards a country threatened with conquest, and it involved adopting the rites of the American Episcopalian Church, which, as a member of the worldwide Anglican Communion, preserves the words and rituals of the Book of Common Prayer, though severed from the central place in politics, society and culture enjoyed, at the time, by the Church of England. It is interesting that it is the Episcopalian Church that is now causing the break-up of the Anglican Communion, by its refusal to endorse Christian teaching on sexuality.

The longing for old England and the Anglican settlement was not absent, even from those who had spent their lives betraying their country. As is so often the case, repudiation is the mark of a love that has become arrested in the stage of disappointment, and which has not learned to forgive. This is amply displayed in the character of Guy Burgess, the most dangerous of the Cambridge spies who, after his escape to Moscow, spoke to his visiting friends constantly of England and her virtues, and asked that after his death his ashes be scattered in an English garden – a request carried out by his brother. (This little episode is the subject of a nostalgic one-act play by Alan Bennett – *An Englishman Abroad*.)

Through all these traumas of the English elite, the Anglican Church stayed where it was, at the centre of our constitution. But it had been transformed from within. It no longer represented the spiritual heart of the nation, and its Archbishop was no longer clearly identified with the English settlement. He had become head of a worldwide Anglican Communion, whose identity and beliefs were hostage to social and cultural changes over which the English Archbishop and Synod could exert no control. At the time when Stalin's agents were recruiting the English upper echelons, the Archbishop of Canterbury (William Temple) was preaching the cause of Christian socialism, and George Orwell was defending a gentle and undeceived English patriotism in which religion played no part. It seemed as though the Anglican Church had been entirely displaced from the centre of English culture, and that its constitutional privileges were a kind of 'rotten borough' in Parliament. In such circumstances it was natural to ask what Anglicanism could possibly stand for, and the question remains today.

In 1870 an American Episcopalian, William Reed Huntington, had proposed four aspects of the Church as defining the unity of the Anglican Communion: the acceptance of the Holy Scriptures as containing all things necessary to salvation; the Nicene Creed as the sufficient statement of the faith; the Sacraments of Baptism and Holy Communion as initiated by Christ himself; and 'the Historic Episcopate, locally adapted to the needs of various regions and peoples'.[49] Huntington's proposal was adopted by the General Convention of the American Church in 1886, and by the Committee of Home Reunion of the Lambeth Conference (which advises the Archbishop) in 1888. Now known as the 'Lambeth Quadrilateral', the four 'pillars' of Anglicanism say nothing specific about the liturgy, and describe the Episcopate as an 'historic' rather than an 'apostolic' succession. Nor, inevitably, do they mention the Act of Supremacy or the relation of the Church to the English Crown.

In so far as there is an official definition of the Anglican Church, however, they provide it.

Yet, while the Quadrilateral probably fairly represents the normal beliefs of moderate Anglicans around the world, it makes no mention of the presence of our Church in the national life. It has nothing to say about the Book of Common Prayer, or about the connection of the Church to British institutions and the Westminster Parliament. And what it offers, by way of faith, is Holy Scripture only. There is no equivalent of the Roman Catholic Magisterium, in which the revelations granted in the Bible are interpreted and integrated by an ongoing stream of philosophical argument. There is no clear statement of what we should do or think when we encounter some passage from the Bible that contradicts either another Biblical passage or something that we know to be true. In effect, the Quadrilateral leaves the various Churches within the Communion to work things out for themselves, while marginalizing the cultural identity of the English Church – the one aspect of it that still called to the English and American elite across the twentieth-century wastelands.

Moreover, it is not at all clear that the Quadrilateral is now accepted by the Episcopalian Church of America, which rejects Biblical teachings on sexuality and marriage, and has made a point of 'moving with the times', regardless of whether the times have much interest in moving with the Church. The English Church has been tempted in the same direction and – partly because of its social and political outreach – believes that it must be 'relevant', though never entirely sure what is relevant or why. The pressure for change here does not come from the Anglican congregations, but from the hierarchy of the Church. It is priests and bishops who have pressed the Church to allow the ordination of women and the solemnization of homosexual unions, for example.

Ordinary churchgoers, in America as in Britain, probably have little desire for those reforms, and may see the Church as having a duty to resist them. Some American Episcopal churches are indeed now affiliating to churches in Africa, in order that their ordinations should be valid in the eyes of their congregations. Others are tempted by the 'ordinariate' of Pope Benedict, inviting them into communion with Rome on terms that will permit their liturgical traditions, while safeguarding their apostolic claims.

These controversies exemplify the essential weakness of the Anglican compromise today. The Church has sat at the centre of an ever-expanding web of toleration, allowing legal recognition to Baptists, Quakers, Methodists, Independents, Presbyterians and Roman Catholics, and making provision in our time for the religions of immigrants coming to Britain from Hindu, Sikh, Buddhist and Muslim societies. But it has assumed that the many churches and creeds with which it seeks to coexist can draw on a common morality and a common allegiance, that they will not prise our country free from the Christian faith or encourage a moral order that is critically at variance with that invoked in the Gospels and the Book of Common Prayer. A national church draws upon another form of membership than that offered through its communion: it is not the face of the community but the halo around that face, which is the face of a country, a jurisdiction and a culture rooted in a place and moving with the times.

The Roman Catholic Church does not face this problem. It defines itself through its apostolic entitlement, its rituals and its Magisterium, and calls to its following from a point beyond their immediate earthly community. Christians who find themselves at odds with the surrounding culture, who cannot in conscience embrace secular values or submit to rituals and liturgies that seem to them to be caricatures of the sacraments and attempts to bring God down to the level of his creatures, instead of ways of raising them to him – such Christians can join the Roman Catholic Communion, without adjusting their secular allegiance. They need only regard themselves as Christians living in a pagan society, like the first disciples of Christ, obedient to God in spiritual matters, and to Caesar in the things of this world. It is for this reason that so many Anglicans since the time of the Oxford Movement have felt the pull of Rome. And Pope Benedict's invitation to Anglican congregations to 'come over', retaining their liturgy and their democratic customs, while enjoying the validation of their priesthood from the Holy See, will exacerbate this tendency. Especially in America, it seems, Anglican congregations are unlikely to remain long in the Protestant camp.

The situation is not uncomfortable for the pure believer only. Fellow travellers find it even more difficult to deal with, for the reason that they accept, perhaps more deeply than committed Christians, the intertwining of secular and spiritual allegiance that is embodied in the Church of England. Wherever you look in our serious post-war culture – Britten's Church Parables, the paintings of David Piper and David Inshaw, the poetry of John Betjeman,

Ted Hughes, Geoffrey Hill and C. H. Sisson, the novels, essays and children's books of C. S. Lewis, the crime fiction of P. D. James, the plays of Alan Bennett and Tom Stoppard – you find the image of England held in an Anglican frame. Even the new literature for children conforms to this rule. J. K. Rowling's Hogwarts, for all its pagan accessories, is an Anglican institution, as Gothic a settlement as any chaplain-haunted public school. Philip Pullman's anti-Narnia, designed as an answer to C. S. Lewis's Christian allegories, takes off from a very Anglican-seeming Oxford college, and at every point recalls the enchanted world of Milton and the struggle of the angels by which our Puritan ancestors thought themselves surrounded. You cannot read very far in English literature, listen very long to serious English music, or walk with your eyes open about our towns and countryside without noticing that an enormous cultural effort has been expended on endowing England with an aura of home and redemption, and that the art devoted to this cause has leaned at every point upon a church that was doing the same.

Hence we should not be surprised that, when the Church of England began to experiment with 'alternative services' in the seventies – a move that was then as formally illegal as hymn singing at the time of Isaac Watts – it was the fellow-travelling intellectuals who made the most noise on behalf of Cranmer's great gift to our nation. The Prayer Book Society, founded in order to ensure that the book was used at least sometimes in the Church that had been built upon it, had the support of an array of secular intellectuals, including Christian agnostics such as Iris Murdoch and Alan Bennett, and the non-believing Jew Isaiah Berlin. For the lover of

literature to describe the new services as 'alternatives' to Cranmer
is like describing *EastEnders* as an 'alternative' to Shakespeare, or
Lady Gaga as an 'alternative' to Bach. But of course, that is an
aesthetic judgement, one that could be made by an outsider to the
religion, for whom faith and worship are not in question. And the
priest whose calling has placed him in an urban parish, surrounded
by people of many beliefs and none, and who must nevertheless
provide for the needs of those for whom the Church is still God's
house in a randomized world, may reasonably believe that he cannot
fulfil his duty by pronouncing words so remote from the daily experience of his flock, or by singing hymns composed in a musical
language that long ago went out of vernacular use.

And again, in this controversy, the English Church has been
more hampered than helped by its constitution. While the
seventeenth-century Church used its legal and constitutional
powers to protect its liturgy and sacramental traditions from the free
experiments of the godly, the twenty-first-century Church is now
using its powers to marginalize those who wish at all costs to hold
on to what it stood for. An illustrative case is that of the parish
church of St Basil, in a Dorset hamlet with the Trollopian name of
Toller Fratrum. In 1981 the church was threatened with closure by
the diocesan authorities in Salisbury unless its congregation agreed
to be amalgamated with those of two nearby parishes, which, unlike
Toller Fratrum, were 'moving with the times'. It was then again
threatened with closure if it did not agree to use the Alternative
Service Book instead of the Book of Common Prayer. During the
nineties the congregation declared that it could not in conscience

accept women priests, and – faced with a newly appointed vicar who plays keyboards in a pop group (Dogs Without Collars) and who wishes to liven up the services with 'relevant' music – finally declared unilateral independence, conducting its own services at times chosen by the congregation, and using the Book of Common Prayer, the King James Bible, the *English Hymnal*, and the forms and ceremonies that were once regarded as uniquely legal and which are now all but forbidden by the guardians of relevance. Thus has a new kind of Congregationalism emerged, one hoping to protect the Anglican Communion from the Church that was designed to impose it.

The Prayer Book Controversy has dwindled but not disappeared. For the Book of Common Prayer belongs, if I am right, to the essence of the Anglican settlement, and not to a passing phase that we have now outlived – in just the way that the Latin Mass belongs to the essence of the Roman Catholic Church. The vandalization of the Anglican liturgy occurred, interestingly enough, at about the same time as the jettisoning of the Latin Mass, and in both cases we see the mark of a disaffected priesthood, unable, without a sense of humiliating theatricality, to perform the traditional rites and ceremonies of the Church. New translations of the Bible and new hymnals emerged in tandem with the new services, the whole amounting to what many saw not merely as an aesthetic disaster, but as a doctrinal heresy. For a sacramental church is not just a place where people get together to announce their adherence to a set of laws, or to bone up on the principles of Biblical theology. It is a place where people come to encounter God, to stand in his presence, and to look with renewed awe on the troubling fact of their own existence, and on the need to be in everyday life what they perforce must be in church – humble members of the Body of Christ.

Sacraments deliver another kind of doctrine from that which can be expressed in the neutral language of theology. Those who see the controversy over the Prayer Book as 'merely aesthetic' are right – except that the word 'merely' misrepresents what is finally at stake. We seek for beauty in our lives because we know that beautiful things are meaningful – though with a meaning that cannot be put into words, since it is communicated directly or not at all. In a similar way we seek for sanctity in our lives because we know that sacred things are also meaningful. Their meaning lies beyond our attempts to express it, and must be experienced directly, in the moment of encounter with the divine presence. The beautiful and the sacred are adjacent in the human psyche, and to neglect or abuse the one is to neglect and abuse the other. Hence liturgical words work on us as poetry works: not by spelling out what (if spelled out literally) would be the bald tenets of a system of belief, but by transporting us beyond the things of this world, into the timeless and placeless presence of the Creator. We are here to kneel, 'where prayer has been valid', and where it will be valid forever if the sacrament is administered.

The shared sense of belonging that defined our country has been eroded from within by changes that we can neither predict nor control. Our Church cannot survive as it did in the eighteenth century, as a leisured precinct in which enlightened clergymen pursued their genial hobbies. It offers its sacraments to a population that lives without rites of passage, and which regards the National Health Service rather than the National Church as its true spiritual guardian. It is the forlorn trustee of an architectural and artistic inheritance that, for all the rampages of the Puritan iconoclasts, remains one of the treasures of European civilization. It is a still point in the centre of our culture, and its defining texts – the King James Bible and the Book of Common Prayer – are the sources from which our self-understanding derives. Yet for most people now resident in England the Church is simply the empty Gothic building at the end of the road, visited for the first time, if at all, when dead.

FIVE

Draw Near With Faith

When T. S. Eliot told her of his conversion to Anglicanism Virginia Woolf expostulated that he had gone mad. She held the orthodox Bloomsbury opinion that one might convert to Roman Catholicism or to communism, since both were ways of rejecting England. But for a modern intellectual to become a believing member of the English Church was a transgression of sacred boundaries, like eating the family dog.

When I let slip among my intellectual acquaintances that I am an Anglican I am often greeted by a similar reaction. How can an intelligent person today sign up to the Christian credo, and how especially can he sign up to it in the context of a national church? I recognize that the previous chapters place on me an obligation to answer that question, and I shall do so as briefly as I can.

My faith unites me to people whose thoughts and feelings I cannot hope to emulate. It unites me to believers like C. S. Lewis, R. S. Thomas and J. R. R. Tolkien. But it also unites me to doubters like Philip Larkin and Benjamin Britten. It unites me, in its way, to Thomas Hardy, whose visionary poem 'God's Funeral' announced the end of Christian belief, and to George Orwell, whose *1984* gave the first full description of what a desacralized world would look like. It unites me to Ralph Vaughan Williams, Graham Sutherland and Paul Nash. Some of those were atheists, some agnostics. Only a minority of them accepted Christ as one Person of the Holy Trinity and the living Word of God. But all accepted the premise from which the Anglican dispensation begins, which is that our being here is mysterious, that we will always fail to explain it, but that we can make in this place of exile a durable and consoling home, one example of which has been England.

The fear of the Lord is the beginning of wisdom, says the Book of Proverbs. By 'fear' I understand awe, humility and a sense of my own powerlessness. I accept Kant's proof of the limits of human reason, and recognize that we cannot extend our concepts so far as to furnish ourselves with an explanation of the world or a concrete knowledge of its Creator. I see the Hebrew Bible as an inspired attempt to comprehend the purposes of a transcendent God, by people who did not really believe him to be transcendent. The book tells the story of a God who is constantly hiding from those who seek him, and whose revelations are granted as though arbitrarily and without giving the recipient the chance to prepare himself. The story of the Old Testament is of a game of hide and seek, but a tragic game, in which God and his people drift further and further apart.[50]

But the New Testament tells another story altogether – the story of a God who reveals himself, not in arcane utterances and inscrutable laws, but as a human being. Christians believe that this human being is identical with the Son, who is one Person of the triune God who sent him. But they also accept that the Trinity is in part a mystery, which cannot be spelled out in literal terms and which stands proxy for profound intuitions concerning the nature of God and the kind of love that God encompasses.

Some Christians follow St Anselm, whose remark *'credo ut intel- ligam'* – I believe in order to understand – puts faith before reason in the scheme of things. The Protestant streak in me tells me to understand first, and let belief come later, when I know what I am being asked to accept. But I also know that there are many things that are entirely real and unquestionable, but which lie beyond my capacity to explain them. That there is something rather than nothing, that there is self-consciousness, that I am free, that the world is law-governed and knowable – all these things are true but inexplicable, since the understanding stops at their threshold, unable to rise to the transcendental perspective from which they might be fully grasped. The creation of something out of nothing is unintel- ligible to us, as is the nature of the Person who can perform such a feat. Likewise the appearance of that Person among us is not some- thing that we can explain in words: it is a mystery of the same order as that of creation.

Although those are things that we do not understand, they correspond, nevertheless, to our religious intimations. We human beings are thrown down in this world without an explanation. The question 'Why am I?' receives no answer from science, or from the normal workings of rational argument. Yet it is an unavoidable by-product of the moral life: it arises just as soon as we recognize that we are bound to each other and to the world by ties of responsibility, that we must account for our actions, and that our lives are worthless until we learn to love and to give.

We must, therefore, see the world as a whole in the terms that are thrust upon us by the moral life. We cannot escape guilt, because we cannot escape judgement. The religious life is one lived in the full consciousness of judgement, and it requires a constant search for absolution – for the cleansing of the soul that comes when the fault is atoned for and forgiven. We can most easily accomplish this if we recognize that the world is a gift and our life a part of that gift. We are called upon to give thanks and the being whom we thank is the one who also grants absolution, since our faults are forms of ingratitude, failures of love. That is the meaning of the two commandments that Christ put above all others and on which 'hang all the law and the prophets' (Matthew 22, 40).

The Roman Catholic Church is right to regard penance as a sacrament. Penance is the work of restoration, which renews and purifies the sinner by putting him once more in a relation of love. It requires the sinner to face up to his failings, to confess to them, to humble himself before God and to make atonement. There are many things wrong with modern societies, but nothing more wrong, it seems to me, than the loss of the habit of repentance. All that is most gross and offensive in the world in which we live comes from the inability of people to live in judgement, to accept the need for remorse and atonement, and to accept that, in begging forgiveness, they must also offer it. All of Christian doctrine points to that process, and when Calvin removed penance from the list of sacraments, he made the first and fatal step towards the de-Christianization of the world.

Our Church has neither followed Calvin nor opposed him. Instead it has buried the question of the sacraments, as it has buried so much else, in the folds of its supplicating rituals. In the Litany and Holy Communion, as these appear in the Book of Common Prayer, confession, repentance and the humble acknowledgement of fault are the substance from which the rites are composed. The congregation is invited to Communion with the following words:

> Ye that do truly and earnestly repent you of your sins, and are in love and charity with your neighbours, and intend to lead a new life, following the commandments of God, and walking from henceforth in his holy ways: Draw near with faith, and take this Holy Sacrament to your comfort; and make your humble confession to Almighty God, meekly kneeling upon your knees.

After confessing their faults and following the age-old rhythm of the Mass to the moment at the altar, the congregation recites the words of humble access:

> We do not presume to come to this thy Table, O merciful Lord, trusting in our own righteousness, but in thy manifold and great mercies. We are not worthy so much as to gather up the crumbs under thy table. But thou art the same Lord, whose property is always to have mercy: Grant us, therefore,

gracious Lord, so to eat the flesh of thy dear Son Jesus Christ, and to drink his blood, that our sinful bodies may be made clean by his body, and our souls washed through his most precious blood, and that we may evermore dwell in him and he in us.

Those tremendous words bring us to the crux; in offering the bread the priest says, 'The Body of our Lord Jesus Christ', and in offering the wine likewise, 'The Blood of our Lord Jesus Christ'. And yet we are not to think of this as a transubstantiation, a coming down of Christ into the stuff that we swallow, but rather as a raising up of ourselves, so that we become members of Christ, who have 'duly received these holy mysteries'. (As Hooker puts it, on the authority of St Paul, the Real Presence is not in the sacrament but in the receiver of the sacrament.[51]) And then, by way of commentary, the congregation says the Gloria, with the wonderful invocation of the 'Lamb of God... that takest away the sins of the world': *agnus Dei, qui tollis peccata mundi*, words that Palestrina, Byrd, Bach, Mozart, Haydn, Verdi and a hundred lesser men have so fully explained in music that it is surely neither necessary nor possible for me to add to what we know.

A sacrament is something that becomes plain to us in the experience of it, but which cannot be translated into prosing sentences. Of course, there are doctrines that form the scaffolding on which the ritual is erected. But they are doctrines to be experienced, and not just believed. We must know in our hearts that we are commanded to love, that we have fallen short and can yet be restored. I am persuaded by the arguments developed over many years by René Girard, who reminds us that the experience of the sacred is peculiar to human beings, and that the sacred and the sacrificial have the same moral root. The sacrificial victim is, for Girard, the paradigm case of the sacred object, the presence among us of 'that which does not belong', whose death purges us of our resentments, and so brings peace.

Long before the Christian revelation that point was understood – understood as *need*, not doctrine. The Scapegoat, the *pharmakon*, he who is both the disease and the cure, would be singled out and sacrificed, in order that those who willed his suffering and inflicted it should overcome their mutual resentments. The habit of ritual murder, which has been a recurring feature of the human condition, stems from the deep need of human beings to project their animosities onto some innocent victim, one who is 'outside the community' and who can, therefore, be attacked without guilt and killed without inviting revenge. The essence of the Christian revelation is that it is for *us* to acknowledge our resentments and to seek forgiveness for them. It is not the victim that should be sacrificed but we ourselves. Spiritual freedom comes from the recognition that we are called upon to give and not to take, to love and not to resent, to make sacrifices and not to impose them. Christ was the sacrificial victim who accepted his role and who went through with it in a spirit of forgiveness. He showed us what is possible, and led us to see that life can be lived as a gift and in a spirit of love. That this is the meaning of the universe, the reason and purpose of its being, is not something that we can prove, and certainly not something that is amenable to argument. But it is revealed to us in Christ's sacrifice, and that is what we mean by his oneness with the Creator.

But what of the after-life? 'If in this life only we have hope of Christ,' wrote St Paul in the First Epistle to the Corinthians, 'we are of all men most miserable.' And in this he expressed the sentiments of all subsequent Christian movements. It seems that, in America at least, the vast majority of people believe in life after death, and that this belief forms an immovable part of the religious package.[52] Yet of all the Christian doctrines that have been discussed, amended and imposed down the ages, the promise of 'eternal life' is intellectually the most challenging. It flies in the face of all we know about our animal nature, all we have observed of the natural world, and all that we could possibly mean by the identity of the person. There is a sense in which my own death is inconceivable – since conceiving brings with it the very self-consciousness that death is supposed to extinguish. My death remains beyond my grasp – I cannot grasp it as *mine*.[53] Yet I only have to reflect on the death of others in order to recognize that my inability to conceive of my death will not prevent it from happening.

Schopenhauer wrote brilliantly and scornfully of the Christian view of the after-life, and of the Last Judgement that distributes rewards and punishments out of all proportion to our meagre deeds.[54] Reading about the Koranic 'Last Day' and what the soul can then expect, Christians often feel a similar scorn. Seventeenth-century Protestants felt the same scorn for the doctrine of Purgatory, invented, they supposed, in order to give the Whore of Babylon another claim on our earthly resources, by selling indulgences and Masses for the dead. Dante's descriptions of Hell and Purgatory illustrate a moral, but do not describe a fact. Only in the *Paradiso* does Dante touch on what eternity might be like, and of course it is like nothing. The poet's longing, drawn by the smile of Beatrice, passes through that smile into the realm of eternal love, where all individuality dissolves, and the soul blends with the *'luce intellettual, piena d'amore'* that is the goal and resolution of our striving. This Platonic vision, in which eternity is earned at the cost of individual existence, offers nothing to the ordinary person who wants to pass through death 'to the other side', and there wake up to a hearty breakfast, with everything proceeding as planned.

In a striking recent work the philosopher Mark Johnston reviews the many arguments, from the Catholic Aquinas, through the Protestant Locke to modern secular philosophers such as Derek Parfit, and concludes that we survive death, not as individuals, since even the resurrection of the body will not secure that result, but as part of the 'onward rush of humankind'.[55] He accepts the Buddhist doctrine of *anatta*, that the self is finite, mortal and bound for extinction. But, Johnston suggests, we live on through *agape*, through the love that unites us with our successors. And for Johnston this is sufficient proof that we really can, through our moral efforts, survive death, that nothing more is needed to justify belief in the after-life, or to find the ground and vindication of the Christian worldview. It is literally true that, through loving your neighbour as yourself, you vanquish your mortality.

I am not confident that Johnston has refuted either the traditional Christian or the atheist perspective. What is important, however, is his emphasis on hope. Christians have a duty to hope, and this hope must, in whatever form, reach beyond the bounds of our earthly life, to engage with the final meaning of the Cosmos. Kant, who argued that the claims of rational theology are unintelligible, nevertheless believed that we must hope for eternal life, and that this hope is present, as it were by implication, in every truly moral act. I am tempted by that idea, and equally by the view that eternity does not come *after* anything, and therefore not after death. And I agree with Schopenhauer that there is something miserable and demeaning in the view that our moral conduct in this life is based on our selfish interests in the next. 'Next' has nothing to do with it: for the time being, I am content to leave the matter there. And I echo the words of Socrates, as he awaited his death: 'I am in hope that there is something for us in death, and as was claimed of old, something better for the good than there is for the bad' (*Phaedo*, 63c).

Seeing the Christian religion in that demythologized way, however, the Church becomes an essential part of it. The essence of the faith is the sacrament, which renews in us not only the spirit of love and forgiveness but also the 'peace of God which passeth all understanding'. This sacrament is essentially a communal celebration, which we understand as joining us together in a community that includes not the living only but also the unborn and the dead. The Anglican rite refers to the 'communion of the saints', meaning all those who have achieved the transformation that comes about when gift and love reorder their life. This membership is offered in the Communion service as a transcendent ideal. But it has a temporal image, and it is to the development and perpetuation of this image that the Anglican Church has devoted its labours down the centuries. In the same way that we are joined to the unborn and the dead by those sacrifices that have created our country, and which are commemorated by the monuments that lie all around, so are we joined to them by that greater sacrifice that shines its light down the centuries, through the Church that Christ himself founded as a perpetual memory and re-enactment of his presence.

Those are mystical thoughts, but the genius of the Anglican Church has been to translate them into durable English, and to found upon them a church that has been a fatherly presence in the lives of English-speaking people. In this book I have told some of the story of that Church, in my life, and in the life of our country. I remain attached to the Church of England as a channel through which the Christian revelation has flowed down the centuries, and around which has grown the culture, the national identity and the sense of collective obligation that I share. It beckons to me still, and to turn my back on it, simply because others are doing the same, would be to betray what is most settled in my own religious feelings. The Anglicanism to which I am attached is like Orthodox Judaism and Hinduism – not abstract doctrine but ritual performance, though a performance through which the profoundest truths of human life are enacted and acknowledged. My kind of Anglicanism would not stand up to the interrogating zeal of an ardent Calvinist. It is a quiet, gentle, unassuming faith that makes room beneath its mantle for every form of hesitation. It belongs to that state of mind that Max Scheler called *'Gottwerdung'* – the becoming of God that is also a becoming of the spirit in me, so as to stand for a moment in the light that shines from beyond this world.[56]

But then, how can such a faith endure, when so few of my countrymen adhere to it? The question is not new: it animates the prophetic books of the Old Testament and the Psalms of David. The Book of Common Prayer, therefore, gives a prominent place to the Venite, Psalm 95, so that at every Morning Prayer the congregation will say, 'Forty years long was I grieved with this generation, and said: It is a people that do err in their hearts, for they have not known my ways.' In the world in which we live, Christians are a marginalized and in many places persecuted sect. It is an offence against political correctness to speak out for the Christian faith, just as it is an offence to declare one's love of England and its inherited ways. But Christians are better fitted to endure this than most religious believers. Their model and example is a man who was 'despised and rejected', and although they are commanded to love their neighbour, they also know that the person who commanded this was crucified for doing so.

For Ever and Ever Amen

The Church of England that I have described was the representative of a shared Christian morality, and a worldwide ecumenical communion, and owed its position to a long history of collaboration and contest between a Christian nation and its sovereign Parliament. It was not an evangelical church, and its congregation has now dwindled to a small minority in the country where it was born. But until very recently the Church of England oversaw the rites of passage through which English society renewed itself, conferring Baptism, Confirmation, marriage and funeral rites on a substantial number of the people. It spoke up, in its mild and embarrassed way, for Christian values whenever they were under attack, and played a discreet but observable role in the education of the young, with daily school assemblies everywhere conducted according to its liturgy and embellished with its hymns. Its Bible and Prayer Book were known to almost every English person, and their words were borrowed for each occasion in which the public affirmation of national loyalty was needed.

Since that time momentous changes have removed the

foundation on which our Church was built. English society is no longer explicitly Christian, and our Parliament is no longer sovereign. The unique position of the Church of England depended on the belief that England was an autonomous, largely Christian, nation, regulating its affairs through the Parliament of Westminster. Parliament was supposed to represent a united kingdom, in which due account would be taken of Scotland, Wales and Northern Ireland, but in which the English settlement would provide the central source of political authority. The Church of England depended on that settlement as it depended on the Crown.

However, the English settlement has now disappeared. The Celtic regions have obtained their own legislative institutions, while retaining the right to return members to Westminster. The Welsh, the Northern Irish and the Scots have two votes – one to legislate for themselves, and another to control the English – while the English have only one. Moreover, legislation is now increasingly initiated by unelected judges in the European Court of Justice and the European Court of Human Rights, neither of which institutions has any sympathy towards the Christian concept of 'natural law'. The EU, in its abortive attempts at a 'constitution', has refused to acknowledge the privileged position of Christianity in the history and identity of the European people. The 'foreign minister' of Europe, Baroness Ashton, has recently declined to condemn the persecution of Christians in North Africa and the Middle East, although repeatedly asked to do so by the governments of Italy, Poland and Spain. Our unelected foreign minister is prepared to condemn the persecution of religious minorities, but will not use the word 'Christian' to describe them, even though it is Christians who are – in this as in most cases now – the victims. To single out Christianity for any kind of protection or preferential treatment is to offend the ruling ideology of 'non-discrimination'. Legislation expressive of Christian values is repeatedly condemned by the European Court of Human Rights, which has ruled that the Polish abortion laws violate the 'human rights' of women, while the Italian custom of placing a crucifix in every classroom was recently held to violate the human right to equal concern (a decision subsequently reversed, but nevertheless of a piece with widespread legislative initiatives to ban the display of religious symbols in public spaces).

The new ideology is less ferocious than the sectarian religions that fought each other to a standstill in the seventeenth century. But it is just as determined to triumph. Christianity must be removed from the public sphere, and deprived of its historical privileges in the settlement of Europe. This is particularly evident when it comes to sexual relations. If you adopt a traditional Christian position with regard to homosexual unions, for example, then you must keep quiet about it, or else lose all chance of advancement in the institutions of secular government. When Rocco Buttiglione, a distinguished Italian politician and academic, was proposed as European Commissioner with a portfolio that included civil liberties, the Italian government was forced to withdraw his nomination on account of his explicitly Christian views on homosexuality.[57] In February 2010 a German mother of eight, who objected to compulsory sex education classes that ran counter to her Christian morality, withdrew her nine-year-old son from school. She was sent to prison for eight days.[58]

Like transubstantiation in the seventeenth century, sex has become the test of doctrinal orthodoxy. In 2008 the Anglican Bishop of Hereford was fined £47,345 and ordered by the court to undergo eight days of 'equal opportunities training', for refusing to hire an active homosexual for a position of trust with young people. In another recent English case a respectable man and wife who had acted successfully as foster parents were held to be incompetent to foster any more children on account of their Christian views, which would lead them to teach the wrong attitude towards homosexuality. The high court ruled that the 'right to non-discrimination' on grounds of sexual orientation would be violated by the couple's educational stance, and that this right takes precedence, in the new order of things, over the right to non-discrimination on grounds of religion. The judges added that the duty of the court is to ensure the welfare of the child, and the presumption was that a child placed with devout Christians would be seriously at risk. Such reasoning is characteristic of judgements now handed down by the courts. Rights are invented, not in order to develop some philosophically based concept of natural law, but in order to advance the cause of the new secular morality, from which all vestiges of the religious ethic – the ethic of 'pollution and taboo' – will have been removed, in favour of the new ethic of 'non-discrimination'.

The Christian Churches have not all regarded marriage as a sacrament, and indeed the position of the Anglican Church in this matter has never been clearly defined. Our Church was for many years tasked with the 'solemnization' of all English marriages; but it arose in order to desolemnize the marriage of Henry VIII. 'Solemnizing' is something that humans can do, whereas sacraments can be accomplished only with God's help – God is a party to them, which is why, on the Roman Catholic understanding, a true marriage cannot be undone. For three centuries our Church has created an obfuscation around this issue, often, in more recent times, seeing its role as simply that of bestowing a 'blessing' on unions that are, in themselves, no more than contracts for cohabitation, whose force is that of a secular agreement. Nevertheless, it has been acutely aware that sexual union cannot be regarded as a purely secular matter. Like other churches, the Church of England has made the sexual bond into its own business, the place in human life where it has a role to play in selectively endorsing our erotic adventures.

Erotic love is the experience in which the distinctions between sacred and profane, consecration and desecration, come most vividly to the fore. It is also encompassed and (until recently) controlled by the most important of all rites of passage – the rite of marriage, on which the future of society and the long-term commitment to children ultimately depend. The first step towards the de-Christianization of society is to destroy the sacrament of marriage, to rewrite the vow taken before God as a contract made between people. But destroying marriage as a sacrament does not take us to the goal of a purely secular order. We need to reconfigure sex itself, so that what was once considered as the privileged union from which the next generation proceeds becomes instead a contract for mutual pleasure. Such a contract, if freely entered, can never amount to a sin, and certainly not merely because the parties are of the same sex.

There is a powerful impetus behind this new view of sexuality, just as there was a powerful impetus behind the Protestant view of the Eucharist. By excluding all vestiges of sacramental feeling from the sexual act, the new morality rescues the individual from the one place where the Church lies in wait for him, the one place where he might be tempted to make an offering of his life, and to move beyond the sphere of worldly contracts into that of sacramental vows. In a similar way, by rewriting the Eucharist as a purely symbolic ritual, the Puritans demoted it from a sacramental moment, in which we are raised by ritual to another level of being, to an illustration of doctrine, a piece of religious prose. Transubstantiation was anathema to the Puritan, because it defined the Eucharist as the place where the Church and its rituals lie in wait for us, the place where the individual might surrender to the call of sanctity, and cease to construe his spiritual well-being simply as a matter between himself and God.

I say that, not by way of condemning the new secular morality, but in order to explain why it is that Christianity in Europe is being singled out for rejection. Christians are not actively persecuted – not yet at least. But they receive no protection from the political class, or from legal and educational institutions that once acknowledged their foundation in the Gospel. The *bien-pensant* pronouncements of the Archbishop of Canterbury have done little to reassure English Anglicans that the Church is really prepared to stand up for their beliefs and values against the onslaught of political correctness.

Those beliefs are mocked by the official culture – by the BBC, for example, and by a large number of public intellectuals – with impunity, and we can now assume that they will not receive any special protection from the courts. When we read that an air hostess has been sacked for wearing a crucifix, or a nurse for praying at the bedside of her patient, or a schoolteacher for teaching his class that the world was created, and that in none of these cases will the law take the side of the victim, we simply bow our heads in silence, and recognize that this is the world in which we live.

In all the centuries of their wanderings, through every kind of persecution and trial, the Jews held on to their religion, consecrating their lives as their ancestors had done, using the language, the words and the rituals that had come down to them from the days before the Temple was destroyed. Their achievement would not have been possible without the belief in the sacred nature of the words and rites that they had inherited, and they looked rightly askance on those who would reform, abandon or replace the ritual prayers. Through the Talmud they expressed their historical sensibility – but in the form of a commentary. The Torah, the Sabbath, the feasts and rites, the matter of the Covenant, these things they retained, as things beyond history. And as a result they survived, a moving and tragic testimony to the beauty of human endurance.

We Anglicans could perhaps retain our religion if we followed the example of the Jews, regarding the texts, rites and feasts as bestowed on us by covenant and not by any earthly settlement. We could set up our own churches, in which to take refuge from the storm of secular orthodoxy, and to comfort each other in the face of the world's contempt. And maybe we could then go on like the Jews, defending our spiritual identity and our special obedience until the end of time. In doing so, however, we would cease to be Anglicans and instead become Congregationalists, with each church managing its own affairs, and perhaps petitioning, now the Pope, now some African bishop, to validate its ordinations. This seems to be what Pope Benedict is now proposing in the 'ordinariate' offered to disaffected Anglicans, and I can understand why American Episcopalian churches should feel the attraction of his call.

But somehow, Toller Fratrum notwithstanding, I don't see that this solution is available to the English. We are bound in a web of interwoven loyalties. Spiritually, politically, even visually and musically our Church has been set down on the land like an all-encompassing spiritual tent, its position secured by subtle straps of law and custom. Our situation is like that of the Hellenistic pagans described by Eunapius, and defended by him against the sacrilegious Christian rabble who were pulling down the temples, insulting their priestesses and sneering at the holy liturgies that had been sung for centuries and whose melodies haunted the land.[59] Although a Christian, I am on the side of Eunapius. But I learn from him that the doctrine of 'non-discrimination', which is not a religion and which therefore cannot last as religions last, will have its time of destruction and will leave the landscape bare. I also learn from Eunapius that *sub specie aeternitatis*, this cannot truly matter, since everything temporal must pass. And then I reflect with gratitude that the English have enjoyed a temporal institution through which, here and there, in whatever mood of penitence or exaltation, an ordinary sinful person could stand at 'the point of intersection of the timeless / With time' and know, from that sublime perspective, that 'History is now and England'.

Notes

1   Arnold Van Gennep, *Les rites de passage*, Paris, 1909.

2   Fetishism, as Kant called it, is therefore not a form of religious faith, but a counterfeit version of it. See *Religion within the Limits of Reason Alone*, pp. 177–9 (original pagination).

3   Words of St Louis de Montfort, adopted as his motto by Pope John Paul II. The 'tu' in question is the Virgin Mary.

4   It is important that in the Muslim cry of devotion, *allahu akbar*, it is the comparative (*akbar*) and not the superlative (*'l-akbar*) that is used.

5   *Either / Or*, 1843, vol. 2, 'The Balance between the Ethical and the Aesthetic', tr. D. F. and L. M. Swenson, Princeton, 1959.

6   *Gulliver's Travels*, Part IV, A Voyage to the Country of the Houyhnhnms.

7   *Les formes élémentaires de la vie religieuse*, Paris, 1912.

8   For a related view see Vladimir Jankélévitch, *Le pur et l'impur*, Paris, 1960.

9   R. Girard, *La violence et le sacré*, Paris, 1972.

10 See the classic study by the Swedish Protestant theologian Anders Nygren, published in English as *Agape and Eros*, 2 vols., London, 1932.

11 'Abd al-Jabbar, *Tathbit dala'l nubuwwat*.

12 See *The West and the Rest*, Wilmington, Delaware, 2002.

13 *The West and the Rest, op. cit.*

14 Max Scheler, *Das Ressentiment im Aufbau der Moralen*, 1912, tr. W. H. Holdheim, New York, 1973. Scheler's views, in this and other works, exerted a powerful influence on Pope John Paul II.

15 F. W. Maitland, *Selected Essays*, London, 1911, p. 129.

16 It has been argued that the idea of a privileged relation between the English and their God precedes the Reformation by centuries. See J. W. McKenna, 'How God became an Englishman,' in D. J. Guth and J. W. McKenna, eds., *Tudor Rule and Revolution*, London, 1982, pp. 25–43.

17 *The Tree of Life*, London, 1943, p. 28.

18 *Essays*, p. 544.

19 The story is told in Anne Hudson, *The Premature Reformation: Wycliffite Texts and Lollard History*, Oxford, 1988.

20 Sir Geoffrey Elton, *England under the Tudors*, Cambridge, 1955.

21 Such was the ground of the vehement denunciation of Henry's attack on the religious orders by Coleridge in *On the Constitution of Church and State*, 1830.

22 Lancelot Andrewes, *Ninety-six Sermons*, vol. 2., Oxford, 1841, p. 296.

23 See Christopher Hill, *The English Bible and the Seventeenth-Century Revolution*, London, 1993.

24 *Life of Milton: English Men of Letters*, London, 1879, p. 69.

25 *Leviathan*, Part 1, ch. 12, Oxford, 2008, p. 71.

26 John Wesley, 'Catholic Spirit', in *The English Sermon*, vol. 3, 1750–1850, ed. Robert Nye, Manchester, 1976, p. 55.

27 See the discussion of the Eucharist in John Lucas, *Essays on Freedom and Grace*, London, 1973, pp. 112–3.

28 The grammar of the old Lord's Prayer (which dates from Cranmer's liturgy of 1549) was already antiquated in 1662, when the Book of Common Prayer as we know it was finally imposed.

29 *The Spectator*, no. 458, 15 August 1712.

30 *The Lion and the Unicorn*, in *Essays*, ed. John Carey, London, 2002, p. 295.

31 *The Tablet*, 25 September 1852, p. 617.

32 Erik Routley, *Hymns and Human Life*, London, 1952, p. 70.

33 Evidently of plainsong origin, though transcribed 'from a French missal' by Thomas Helmore (1811–90).

34 And used again by René Girard, in the title of his important book on scapegoating and victimization, *Des choses cachées depuis la fondation du monde*, Paris, 1978.

35 *Laws of Ecclesiastical Polity*, Book V, ch. 67, section 7.

36 See Ronald Knox, *Let Dons Delight*, London, 1939, a classic exploration of the dilemmas facing an established church as the common culture of Christianity disintegrates. Knox's *Spiritual Aeneid, Being an Account of a Journey to the Catholic Faith* (1918) summarizes the motives and feelings of a whole generation of converts from Anglicanism.

37 *Impressions that Remained*, 2nd edn, vol. 1, London, 1919, p. 57.

38 Thomas Hughes, *Tom Brown's Schooldays*, 1857.

39 Georges Bataille, *L'érotisme ou la mise en question de l'être*, Paris, 1957.

40 *Death-Devoted Heart: Sex and the Sacred in Wagner's Tristan und Isolde*, Oxford, 2003.

41 Werner Jaeger, *Paideia*, 3 vols., London, 1939.

42 Lytton Strachey, *Eminent Victorians*, London, 1918.

43 Richard Deacon, (pseudonym for Donald McCormick), *The Cambridge Apostles: A History of Cambridge University's Elite Intellectual Secret Society*, London, 1985.

44 See in general the life of E. W. Benson by Geoffrey Palmer and Noel Lloyd, *Father of the Bensons*, Harpenden, 1998.

45 On Benson's life see Brian Masters, *The Life of E. F. Benson*, London, 1991.

46 'What I Believe', published in *The Nation*, 16 July 1938.

47 Cyril Connolly, *Enemies of Promise*, London, 1938.

48 See especially the essays in T. S. Eliot, *For Lancelot Andrewes*, London, 1928, and W. H. Auden, *The Dyer's Hand*, London, 1962.

49 *The Church-idea: An Essay Towards Unity*, New York, 1870.

50 See Jack Miles, *God: a Biography* (New York, 1995), which tells the story from God's perspective.

51 *The Laws of Ecclesiastical Polity*, Book V, ch. 47.

52 2003 survey by the Barna Research Group.

53 On this point see the subtle and detailed argument of J. J. Valberg, *Dream, Death and the Self*, Princeton, 2007.

54 *Parerga and Paralipomena*, vol. 2, no. 177.

55 Mark Johnston, *Surviving Death*, Princeton, 2010.

56 *Die Stellung des Menschen im Kosmos*, Darmstadt, 1928.

57 Just what *is* the Christian position on homosexuality? St Paul's outright disgust is surely not acceptable to the Christian conscience today. But Christianity retains the belief that monogamous sexual union between man and woman is the ideal to which our conduct should tend, or – if we renounce that goal – that we should be chaste. Few of us succeed in this demanding regime, and most take comfort from Christ's wonderful judgement in the case of the woman taken in adultery. On this view, homosexual acts are sinful in the way that non-marital sex is sinful. The troubling question concerns not the act but the desire: is it like incestuous desire, a transgression of sacred boundaries? Or is it simply a natural temptation, to be resisted as best we can? Surely the correct response of a Christian to such a question is the conciliar approach, to seek guidance in council, and not to take refuge in the fierce absolutes of a vanished age.

58 For this and similar cases, see the 'Shadow Report' of the Viennese Observatory on Intolerance and Discrimination against Christians: www.intoleranceagainstchristians.eu.

59 See Eunapius, *Lives of the Sophists*, fourth century AD, a last-ditch attempt to defend the schools of philosophy against Christian ignorance. Then, as now, ignorance triumphed, it being always easier to destroy learning than to maintain it.

About the Author

ROGER SCRUTON is a writer and philosopher who has written on aesthetics, politics, music and architecture. He is Research Professor at the Institute for the Psychological Sciences in Washington and Oxford and is Resident Scholar at the American Enterprise Institute in Washington. His most recent books, *The Uses of Pessimism* and *Green Philosophy*, were published by Atlantic Books.